installation art
in the new millennium

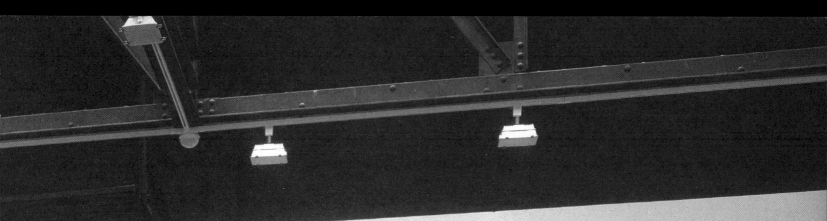

NICOLAS DE OLIVEIRA

NICOLA OXLEY

MICHAEL PETRY

installation art
in the new millennium

the empire of the senses

TEXTS BY NICOLAS DE OLIVEIRA

with 317 illustrations, 269 in colour

contents

page 1 Oswaldo Macia, *Memory Skip*, 1995 The Colombian artist Oswaldo Macia's work straddles the visual and the olfactory. In it smell becomes a physical object. Here, the skip held pine essence and its scent acted as a memory aid, though pine soap is generally used as a cleaning agent and for evacuating noxious odours. The liquid was bound by its solid container, but its odour evaded such fixed parameters and pervaded the entire space. *Memory Skip* was partnered by an audio work entitled *The Sound of Smell*, recorded in a sound studio and consisting of the mechanical grinding and manual chopping of pine needles. This lasted the length of time as it took for the sealed room to be filled with scent.

pages 2–3 Andrea Zittel, *Raugh Furniture: Lucinda*, 1998 (see page 74).

First published in the United Kingdom in 2003 by Thames & Hudson Ltd, 181A High Holborn, London WC1V 7QX

www.thamesandhudson.com

© 2003 Thames & Hudson, Ltd, London

British Library Cataloguing-in-Publication Data A catalogue record for this book is available from the British Library

ISBN 0-500-23808-1

Printed and bound in China by C+C Offset

introduction 12

Over the past decade the position of Installation art has shifted from a relatively marginal practice to achieving mainstream status within contemporary visual culture. Its hegemonic presence has given rise to new terms which redefine the art form and impact on a range of other disciplines.

Artists and works that mark this shift include: Ann Hamilton (USA), Stan Douglas (Canada), Stefan Brüggemann (Mexico), Steven Pippin (UK), Barbara Kruger (USA), Hans Op de Beek (Belgium), Rodney Graham (Canada), Michael Landy (UK), Tomoko Takahashi (Japan), Ilya Kabakov (Russia), Chris Burden (USA) and Francesc Torres (Spain).

escape 49

The new 'immersive' Installation reflects desire for sensual pleasure. It provides a 'total artwork' which envelops the viewer in a hermetic and narcissistic space. The location of the installation is in the realm of the imaginary, stimulated by the need for escape.

Artists featured include Doug Aitken (USA), Per Barclay (Norway), Olafur Eliasson (Denmark), Bruce Gilchrist and Jo Joelson (UK), Ann Veronica Janssens (UK/Belgium), Kazuo Katase (Japan), Jaume Plensa (Spain), Ugo Rondinone (Switzerland), Børre Sæthre (Norway), Andrea Zittel (USA), Lee Bul (Korea) and Pierre Huyghe (France).

author and institution 78

While artists desire autonomy, their installations often require collaborators in the form of museums and curators. The resulting relationships provide a platform for discussion and collaboration. The outcome of this process is the project: Installation as an open-ended experiment which transforms the art institution into a cultural laboratory.

Artists in this section include: Barbara Bloom (USA), Martin Creed (UK), Henrik Plenge Jakobsen (Denmark), Mischa Kuball (Germany), Micah Lexier (Canada), John Newling (UK), Tobias Rehberger (Germany), Navin Rawanchaikul (Thailand), Elmgreen & Dragset (Denmark/Norway) and Thomas Hirschhorn (Switzerland).

exchange and interaction

Installation has been defined by its refusal to accept fixed boundaries. Its experimental edge has led artists to examine the boundaries of other disciplines. Practitioners are looking to forge relationships of exchange with other artists on a global level, through the ability of fast travel, information technology and the media. In addition, Installation artists have found opportunities to collaborate with specialists in areas such as anthropology, science and technology, opening the field to experimental strategies beyond the traditionally visual. Installation is thus seen as moving beyond the physical boundary of a single space into a realm of negotiated interactivity and simultaneity.

Artists are drawn from a broad spectrum of Installation practice and include: Atelier van Lieshout (Netherlands), Jose Dávila (Mexico), Alicia Framis (Spain), Carsten Höller (Belgium), the duo Muntean/Rosenblum (Austria/Israel), Carsten Nicolai (Germany), the Scandinavian group N55, Paola Pivi (Italy), Mark Povell (UK), Allan Wexler (USA) and Keith Tyson (UK).

time and narrative

In a rapidly changing world, time and memory are key concerns for contemporary artists. Though borrowing from existing methodologies, Installation artists prefer to construct their own spaces of memory. The singular term 'history' is under constant threat from the emergence of multiple 'histories'. Artists have used this concern with remembrance by focusing on official and unofficial means of retrieval in an attempt to question existing systems through more private and individual ways.

Examples are drawn from the works of: Christian Boltanski (France), David Bunn (USA), Damien Hirst (UK), Tadashi Kawamata (Japan), the French duo Loriot/Mélia, Mike Nelson (UK), Jason Rhoades (USA), Bob & Roberta Smith (UK), Jane and Louise Wilson (UK), Eija-Liisa Ahtila (Finland) and João Penalva (Portugal).

the body of the audience

Following an examination of the conditions of contemporary viewing, it is argued that the audience has become the key site of the Installation. This chapter concludes that Installation returns us to the body of the spectator, a space that is sentient and active: The Empire of the Senses.

Artists include: Vanessa Beecroft (Italy), Carlos Amorales (Mexico), Thomas Eller (Germany), Gary Hill (USA), Christian Jankowski (Germany), Aernout Mik (Netherlands), Santiago Sierra (Spain), Roman Signer (Switzerland), Christine Hill (USA), Mariko Mori (Japan) and Sylvie Fleury (Switzerland).

foreword
by Jonathan Crary

For the last several centuries, the most compelling forms of Western visual art were often works by artists who critically engaged with the experience of human perception, who tested its limits and expanded its possibilities. The Scientific Revolution accelerated the search for workable explanations for understanding the interplay of vision and appearance, and the empirical study of perception became a recurring part of the modernization of European thought. With the models of artist-researchers like Leonardo and Brunelleschi available, innovative art has frequently taken shape within an awareness of the double-sidedness of perceptual experience: that it is formed both through external techniques and practices and through the subjective capabilities of the observer's own body and nervous system. For many centuries, representational techniques like perspective and printing exemplified the standardization as well as the replication, storage and circulation of perceptual experience, while devices such as the telescope or microscope functioned as prosthetic amplifications and extensions of human sensory capabilities.

Up until the mid-1800s the artist operated within conditions of relative equilibrium between the imperatives of external rules and techniques (e.g. academic codes and studio practices, optical instruments like the Claude Glass, and perspectival systems) on one hand and the autonomy of subjective visual experience on the other. But beginning in the late 19th century, intensified technological development triggered the erosion of this reciprocity between individual experience and exterior processes and instruments. The last 125 years have seen a dramatic transfer of human capabilities to machines, especially capabilities involving vision, thought and memory which continues unabated today, in terms of tools for information storage, communication and visualization. We are now in a material environment where earlier 20th-century models of spectatorship, contemplation and experience are inadequate for understanding the conditions of cultural creation and reception. If the diverse artists featured in this volume have anything in common, it is a recognition of this shift and a realization that art must reconfigure itself in relation to transformed modes of cognition and experience. Their work is linked, directly and indirectly, with the activity and imagination of new groups, subjectivities and communities in a conflict-ridden global environment. Taking place in both art and in diverse cultural arenas are experiments with perceptual and cognitive experiences outside of the dominant possibilities offered by contemporary media and technology. Some of this experimental activity involves the creation of unanticipated spaces and environments in which our visual and intellectual habits are challenged or disrupted. The processes through which sensory information is consumed become the object of various strategies of de-familiarization.

The continuing proliferation of techniques of perception and information is tied to one of the crucial paradoxes of global present: the greater the technological capacity for connection, speed, for exchange and circulation of information, the more fragmented and compartmentalized the world becomes. Much of our intellectual heritage from the Enlightenment supported the opposite belief: that universal access to knowledge and communication tools ought to have been the basis for conditions of freedom and participatory democracy for example. For those working in the visual arts and new media, there is a particular awareness that the current spread of communication networks is not generating a trans-national community with a shared set of aesthetic and perceptual foundations. Instead, there has been the spread of relatively self-sufficient micro-worlds of affect, meaning and experience, between which intelligible exchange is less and less possible.

The unfathomable amount of information available today works powerfully against the possibility or even the ideal of shared knowledge. Instead, electronically accessible data can be used in the service of any point of view, regardless of how extreme or absurd. But it is within this generalized epistemological crisis that some of our most important contemporary artists, grouped here under the term 'Installation art', are rethinking the nature of research, challenging hegemonic uses of media and testing out new ways of assembling and presenting information. We encounter here strategies of materializing knowledge through concrete procedures of bricolage, as well as unexpected awakenings of communal memory within a culture dependent on historical amnesia. This is a far cry from the appropriation art of the 1980s when it was fashionable to present virtuoso demonstrations of endless chains of simulation, of the cynical play of signs and images that supposedly no longer referred to anything.

As the authors of this volume recognize, the appellation 'Installation art' is a paradoxical one in that it too can imply a sense of position and a spatial homogeneity which is alien to most of the examples of work represented here. For, in fact, Installation art directly engages the patchwork, composite character of contemporary experience and it does so with a stunning diversity of materials and practices. In a related sense, 'Globalization' is also a misleading term in that it seems to connote spatiality or territory, albeit on a large scale. But as we well know, the workings of capitalism now are increasingly independent of actual territory. There is more and more disconnection of economic circulation from physical space, as abstract forms of wealth have a mobility and fluidity unrelated to what we used to think of as location. This should not lead us to hyperbolic theories about the disappearance of space or the ubiquity of instantaneous speed and so on. We must begin to understand the strange kind of dislocations and associations that now constitute subjective reality. Unavoidably, our lives are divided between two essentially incompatible milieus; on one hand, the spaceless electronic worlds of contemporary technological culture and, on the other, the physical extensive terrain on which our bodies are situated. Much Installation art affirms that experience (and art) is constituted out of the paradoxes and discontinuities of this mixed heterogeneous zone.

Many of the Installation artists seem to be working with the awareness of how the tangible 'real' world can seem dilapidated in comparison with the infinite phantasmagoria of images and data available on-line or on-screen. The potential decrepitude of our physical surroundings and all the cosmetic, genetic imperfections (not to mention the mortality) of our own bodies are a permanent humiliation in the face of dematerialized digital phenomena. It is of course entirely logical now

that immense corporate industries are relentlessly trading upon the fragility of the body to expand a central arena of consumption: bio-engineering, cosmetic surgery, psycho-chemicals ever more available for diverse emotional and behavioural needs (e.g. an anti-shyness drug now being marketed), anti-aging procedures, and the patenting and commercialization of the human genome, to name a few. But these are some of the issues out of which artists are generating counter-models of the body and its dynamics, which disclose its political volatility and which might work against its fraudulent domestication.

The cultural changes now underway, however, are not analogous to previous historical transformations. The rise of typographic culture did not suddenly occur after the 15th-century invention of the printing press and moveable type. It took place slowly over several centuries and its effects were not fully in place until the late 18th or early 19th centuries in terms of an extensive diffusion across a social field. Perhaps most significantly though, we are not witnessing so much a change in technological conceptions from one dominant arrangement of machinic systems to another, as the emergence of an unprecedented dynamic of continual innovation and obsolescence. It is not as if we are in a transitional period of adjustment to a new set of tools which will all seem quite mundane in another generation, like the telephone or radio. For the vast majority of people, our perceptual and cognitive relationship to communication and information technology is and will continue to be estranged, because the speed at which new products appear and reconfigurations of technological systems take place precludes the possibility of ever becoming familiar with a given arrangement. What we habitually refer to as photography, film, video, television no longer has a stable identity and is now subject to increasingly frequent mutations as part of larger technological transformations. Whatever is currently touted as essential to our practical needs is always disquietingly close to obsolescence. Perception itself is so closely aligned with these rhythms of change that one of its primary characteristics is continual permutation. In this context, aesthetic debates dependent on the notion of 'medium' are out of touch with contemporary actuality. Much of the work documented here consists of provisional counter-strategies of integrating technological tools into plural zones of creative activity, and of inventing flexible models of imagination and narrative outside of the enforced routines of cultural consumption. It establishes a perceptual field which simultaneously engages periphery and centre, continually revealing multiple routes of entry and exit. Perhaps most importantly, the work is often frankly utopian in its ambitions: it provides a rough outline of alternate forms of living, creating and thinking which might become hopeful anticipations of a highly variegated but more egalitarian global future.

Tomoko Takahashi, *Line Out*, 1999
Referring to an unprejudiced
exploration of selection and
classification, a cheerful celebration
of human organizing tendencies,
Takahashi focuses on the retrieval
and redeployment of materials in
order to integrate the detritus of
consumer society into an artistic
practice. She creates chaotic tableaux
of redundant equipment which can be
interpreted as fantasies of neurotic,
urban landscapes.

introduction

In February 2001 the British artist Michael Landy re-opened the disused
C&A department store in London's Oxford Street. Over a period of two
weeks all his belongings were publicly destroyed for his installation
Break Down. In the catalogue of the show Landy provided an inventory
of his posessions: 'Artworks, Clothing, Electrical, Furniture, Kitchen,
Leisure, Motor Vehicle, Perishable, Reading Material, Studio Materials'.
He described the work thus: *Break Down* is a bit like a Scalectrix version
of a material reclamation facility with all my possessions circulating on

Michael Landy, *Break Down*, 2001

a roller conveyor until they are taken apart. I'm building an audit of my life. Objects that have been classified into different categories...are numbered, weighed and detailed on an inventory.... The conveyor is like a plinth in a way, it-er-conveys what's going on.'

Break Down provides a useful departure point for reconsidering the nature and form of the artwork at the beginning of the 21st century as it raises important questions about the current position of the artist, material culture, exhibition practices and the role of the audience in Installation art. This book aims to present the diverse practices that have today come to redefine the term Installation art.

The final decade of the 20th century saw the passage of Installation art from a relatively marginal art practice to the establishment of its current central role in contemporary art. 'These days installation art seems to be everybody's favourite medium,' wrote the influential American critic Roberta Smith in 1993. She was also critical, stating that 'installation has become a series of conventions' (Smith uses the terms 'installation' and 'installation art' interchangeably). However, as we shall see, in the intervening years Installation has moved from what the American art theorist Hal Foster describes as 'medium specific' to 'debate specific', a form of art that is not defined in terms of any traditional medium but in terms of the message it conveys by whatever means.

Earlier attempts to define Installation art by medium alone failed because it is in the nature of the practice itself to challenge its own boundaries. This questioning process constitutes a discourse which investigates the relationships between the artist and the audience. Installation is therefore defined by this process, something that has led artists to work with materials and methodologies not traditionally associated with the visual arts. Roberta Smith's assertion that Installation was governed by conventions has been challenged since the publication of her article. Current practice suggests that a more fluid and open approach has taken over from the conventions that attempted to bind Installation art to the medium. This idea of fluidity was already being discussed in relation to Postmodern practice in the 1980s. Moreover, it is in the current period that these earlier theories have become fully integrated into art practice. As the French philosopher Jean Baudrillard noted: 'The medium is no longer identifiable as such, and the confusion of the medium and the message (McLuhan) is the first great formula of this new era.' The Canadian theorist Marshall McLuhan was one of the key theorists writing in the early 1960s to address the impact that information technology would have on global culture. This formula predicts the shift from objective critique towards a new subjectivity which emphasizes uncertainty and brings both artist and viewer together in a discursive environment.

The practice of the Russian artist Ilya Kabakov has been emblematic of this move from objective knowledge to subjective experience. His *Palace of Projects* (1998) presented a vast range of proposals from the

Ilya Kabakov, *The Palace of Projects*, (detail), 1998

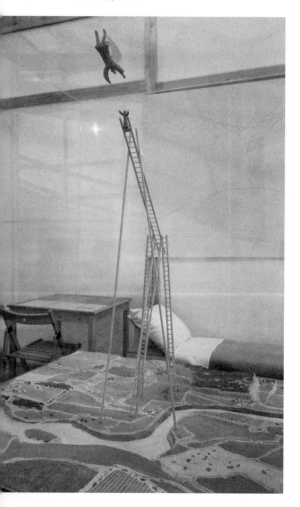

Russian people, which were then turned into maquettes and drawings. These proposals were the flights of fancy of ordinary people faced with the breakdown of ideological certainties in the wake of the collapse of the Soviet Union. Kabakov goes so far as to state that Installation will take the place of 'the icon, the fresco, and the painting'. He affirms that Installation 'is not a movement in art, not a new or fashionable style' but rather 'a new genre which is still in the very beginning of its development.' Kabakov sees Installation as a genre entirely directed towards the viewer, though the audience's reaction is anticipated by the artist. In generating the work, the artist instils a sense of familiarity in the viewer, directing them to their own everyday experience. Moreover, the demystification of art's content in Kabakov's work is a concern shared by many artists.

While referring to the content of Installation art, Rochelle Steiner, curator of the Saint Louis Art Museum, writes that 'museological critique, world and identity politics, and the position of the viewers tend to be preconditions rather than battlegrounds.' These terms, suggested by Steiner, are no longer the subject of installations but constitute a

Francis Alÿs, *When Faith Moves Mountains*, 2002
The Belgian artist Francis Alÿs' work crosses over between performance, painting, photography and web projects. On 11 April 2002, five hundred volunteers were given shovels and asked to form a single line at the foot of a giant sand dune in Ventanilla, an area outside Lima, Peru. This human comb pushed a quantity of sand a specific distance, thereby moving a 16-foot-long (4.8 m) sand dune roughly 4 inches (10 cm) from its original position. The piece functions as a social allegory, infiltrating local history and mythology with the aim of de-romanticizing Land Art.

right Renée Green, *Between and Including*, 1999

opposite left Meschac Gaba, *Museum Shop*, 2001
The Benin artist Meschac Gaba diagnoses how art history and the museum culturally, ethnocentrically and selectively assimilate non-European cultures. The piece Project for the Museum of African Contemporary Art was made in Amsterdam in 1997 at the Rijksakademie. This museum, organized in twelve different departments or installations (Museum Shop, Museum Restaurant, Museum Discotheque, etc.), was reconstructed and temporarily staged for exhibitions. Gaba playfully confronts his work with the defined mechanisms of business and the rules of the global contemporary art market.

common ground between artist and audience upon which the work is based. Installation is therefore not specifically charged with addressing the issues mentioned by Steiner, as artists and viewers already understand these concerns as *given*. In the many contemporary installations that recognize the reality of an information culture the issues are implicit.

Many artists appear to give credence to Steiner's argument; as the issues are implicit in the work, they can remove the need to remind the audience of their presence. The American artist Renée Green constructs video-lounges and libraries which act as information centres in which the viewer becomes a 'browser' who picks from the available material. Similarly, Meschac Gaba from Benin provided a reading area and a shop entitled *Museum Shop* (2001), which invited visitors to browse through books and magazines. Both these artists' installations propose informal settings which encourage spectators to relax and enjoy the work without being pressurized by overt messages or ideological stances. The perceived absence of apparent control mechanisms or the lack of

an explicit message in these works suggests an understanding shared between the artist and the audience. The audience is encouraged to choose its own interpretation without relying on that of the artist. Artists and curators are indeed motivating spectators to experience works in an open-ended manner and become authors and generators of their own meanings.

The relationship between the artist and the audience is closely linked to the continuing debate around 'theatrical space'. If the gallery or site is likened to a stage, the question then arises of how and why the viewer participates in the work. The American curator Robert Storr's exhibition '*Dis*locations' at the Museum of Modern Art in New York in 1992 helped to pave the way for the recognition of Installation art as a mainstream discipline. His article 'No Stage, No Actors, But It's Theatre (and Art)', published in 1999, observed that installations have become 'complete immersion environments'. Refering to installations by artists such as Ilya Kabakov and Ann Hamilton, he asserts that 'the experience they provide is much like wandering onstage and picking up loose pages from a script,

above right Bik Fillingham Van der Pol, *The Bookshop Piece*, 1996
This was a recreation of the theory section of the ICA Bookshop in London at the Museum Boijmans van Beuningen, Rotterdam.
One of the characteristics of the ICA Bookshop is that the main stock consists of theory-related literature, including sociological, cultural, historical and philosophical works. The Dutch artists Liesbeth Bik, Peter Fillingham and Jos van der Pol, who work collaboratively under the name Bik Fillingham Van der Pol, wanted to create a link between the different collections, which operate in discrete areas such as modern art, classical art, prints and design. The reconstruction of the ICA Bookshop was based with the original architect's plans and included all titles on a sale-or-return basis.

right Barbara Kruger, *Power Pleasure Desire Disgust*, 1997
The American artist Barbara Kruger no longer attacks the public's attitudes towards advertising and mass propaganda but their zones of intimacy which create claustrophobic spaces. Her signature texts and aphorisms are projected all over the gallery's surface, while on the rear wall, three large-scale video projections of changing heads voice her confrontational texts, based on snatches of dialogue overheard by the artist.

overhearing bits of recorded dialogue and trying to figure out what the setting is...and what actions might still be taken.' He implies that the proscenium arch has been removed and that the division between actors and audience is no longer clear. The removal of the frame that separates stage from auditorium brings together the spheres of making and viewing. The 'theatricality' of the work, once seen as a weakness because of the reliance on entertaining the audience, has become a virtue. Rochelle Steiner goes so far as to state that 'theatricality paradoxically outlined the conditions that would come to define installation art.'

Yet, while the idea of the theatre still provides one of the paradigms for today's installations, its rhetoric has been superseded by other concerns. In *Double Bind* (2001), the last major work by the Catalan artist Juan Muñoz, the idea of the stage remains present through repeated use of framing devices. The installation at Tate Modern, London, provided a labyrinthine architecture of several levels and chambers and introduced *trompe l'œil* effects which encouraged multiple perspectives. Placed strategically, a series of cast figures, painted the same shade of grey as

opposite Juan Muñoz, *Double Bind*, 2001

above Juan Muñoz, *Double Bind*, 2001

the entire work, stood watching. The Turbine Hall, a cavernous and dramatic space combined with the monumental scale of the work to curtail intimacy and to remove the possibility of a single perspective for the static viewer. However, the theatricality of this installation was placed at the service of a dysfunctional play with the conditions of viewing which emphasized the alienation of the audience.

The British collective Blast Theory have moved away from the constrictions of traditional performative spaces by engaging with the possibilities offered by new technologies. Their 1998 project, *Kidnap*, followed the popular format of Reality-TV where individuals were invited

below Blast Theory, *Kidnap*, 1998

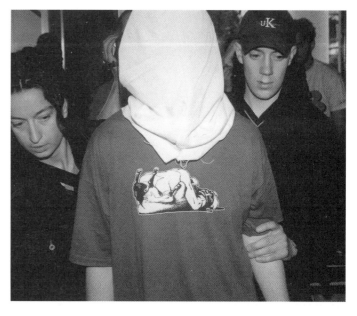

to compete for their own abduction. Two winners were selected and kidnapped by the group then taken to an undisclosed location where their captivity was filmed and could be watched as a live webcast. This project parallels the shift from static notions of space and time towards multiple spaces and simultaneous events, a move closely associated with the development of 'telematic media'. This term is used to describe the range of new tele-technologies that enable us to instantaneously and simultaneously transmit sound and vision to any number of locations. This simultaneity has a disorienting impact on our experience of space and time and has become an important issue in the development of Installation. Moreover, in recent years we have witnessed the arrival of digital technology, as well as the availability of new means of production and reception based around the processing power of the personal computer as a virtual studio. The virtual studio offers new working tools for artists, and encourages a nomadic and heterogeneous practice. The Mexican artist Stefan Brüggemann stated, in conversation with the authors, 'Who needs a studio? All an artist needs today is a computer and a phoneline.' Thus, these technologies have been instrumental in changing the role of the artist from that of a generator of original or primary materials, to that of an editor of existing cultural

left Stefan Brüggemann, *Opening*, 1998 Brüggemann's work challenges the institutional framework, which is continually used for the presentation of visual art. The Mexican artist removed the plate-glass window of the exhibition space from the street elevation, allowing the audience to step through. The window that usually provides the first visual contact with the museum and its contents loses its function as a looking glass, while acquiring a new status as an exhibit.

opposite Wendy Bornholdt, *Subspace SE8 3NU (Relay)*, 2001
The installation by the New Zealand artist Wendy Bornholdt consisted of a walkway of scaffold poles and thin strips of mirror. A cycle of hissing white noise imposed itself on the space, only to be counterpointed by moments of pristine silence. The noise plundered one's ability to concentrate or complete a thought, while the silence was accompanied by an acute awareness of the moment of anticipation when thought could be resumed.

below Ann Hamilton, *Salic*, 1995

objects to be inserted into new contexts. This argument is echoed in the book *Postproduction* by the French curator and theorist Nicolas Bourriaud who likens the activity of the artist to that of the computer programmer or the DJ. 'This recycling of sounds, images, and forms implies incessant navigation within the meanderings of cultural history, navigation which itself becomes the subject of artistic practice.'

The British author J. G. Ballard has extensively explored the shifts in cultural experience as we adapt to new technological landscapes. In an interview with the Italian journalist Lorenza Pignatti he stated: 'Our homes are slowly turning into TV studios, full of electronic equipment – camcorders, VCRs, advanced stereo systems – designed to make us the star, script-writer, director of our own continuing mini-drama. Reality is turning into a home movie, in which an infanticized version of ourselves runs across a garden of artificial grass.' However, though the technologies to which Ballard refers are having a deep impact, transforming the private representation of individual identities and the

environment of the home, the cinematic experience continues to dominate the public language of visual culture. Therefore, in spite of the proliferation of home entertainment, the resurgence of cinema-going since the 1980s reveals a continuing desire for immersion in a communal activity with repetitive conditions. The 'immersive condition', discussed more fully in Chapter 1 (Escape) clarifies why the cinema has been crucial in the development of Installation. Cinema provides the dominant cultural experience that Installation must explore. Film has been instrumental in setting the viewing conditions and expectations for today's audiences, as it envelops the spectator in an overwhelming spectacle of narrative, sound and vision. Despite the escalation of 'special effects', along with the improvements in sound technology and viewer comforts which have helped to fill cinemas, watching films still relies on the traditional division between screen and audience. This separation provides, on the one hand, a practical viewing solution, while on the other, it allows the audience to focus on the narrative or the unfolding of the plot. Installation, through its use of cinematic techniques both quotes and deconstructs the experience of film: its viewing place and conditions, its narrative sequencing and its use of represented space. To this end, artists such as the American Ann Hamilton and the Canadian Stan Douglas have used the effects of early cinema in their installations.

Stan Douglas, set for *Der Sandmann*
(The Sandman), 1995

Jonathan Hernández, *Everything is OK*, 2001
The Mexican artist Jonathan Hernández confronts the viewer with a glittering statement about existence. His work elicits responses from his audiences, asking them to reflect on his statements, which are paradoxically banal and profound.

Hamilton's *Salic* (1995) was staged in a disused passenger carriage and used the pre-cinematic device of the Zoetrope to arrive at flickering projections which simulated the train's movement. Douglas's *Der Sandmann* (1994–97), used two film projectors to create a split-screen effect. Douglas built two identical filmsets of a civic garden, one showing the garden in contemporary times, the other as it would have been in the 1970s. These were filmed using the same 360-degree rotation in a continuous pan and then projected to form two halves of a screen so that one image always appeared to wipe out the other. The resulting installation uses this complex technique to represent the return of repressed memory and history which the Austrian psychoanalyst Sigmund Freud describes in his essay *The Uncanny* (1919). Artists are using the physical apparatus of film-making, the language of cinematography and the subject matter of filmic narrative as a means of exploring the conditions of viewing when film is taken out of the cinema and installed in the gallery context. The British artist Sam Taylor-Wood makes multi-screen films, often casting well-known actors and celebrities, in which the camera is used as a static eye and the action unfolds in front of it. The use of recognizable personalities echoes the position of the film star in cinema. In Taylor-Wood's work the viewer remains unsure as to whether the celebrities are playing a part or are simply themselves. In so doing, the artist reveals the way in which life seeks to imitate film. In contrast, the Swiss artist Ugo Rondinone constructs atmospheric filmic installations which immerse the spectator in a repetitive and purposefully nostalgic dream-state.

The work of the American artist Matthew Barney is emblematic of this confusion of boundaries between disciplines, as he fuses film, installation, theatre and set-design. His epic film cycle *Cremaster* is characterized by lush backdrops, slick art direction and labyrinthine narratives. On questioning one of his actors, Steve Tucker, guitarist

in the band Morbid Angel about *Cremaster 2* (1999), Tucker said:
'Dude, it's unbelievable...I could watch it a thousand times, frame
by frame and never tire of watching it, but still never know completely
what the fuck it was about.' In Barney's work, which operates between
film and installation, the theatrical element is always present. 'Character,
for Barney,' writes art critic Neville Wakefield, 'is sculptural material.'

While Installation was seen as an emerging practice, many attempts
were made to define its ever-growing remit. In the current period,

Matthew Barney, *Cremaster 2:
The Drone's Exposition*, 1999

Alexandra Ranner, *Basement*, 2001
By transforming elements of
photographs or stills from films into
three-dimensional works, the German
artist Alexandra Ranner re-creates
spatial arrangements. These artificial,
model-like replications are often
reminiscent of the anonymity of cheap
hotel rooms and furnished apartments.
The atmospheric suggestion of the
photographic or pictorial view is
transformed into a bodily encounter.

however, artists and curators make use of the term to describe a
wide area of related activities across a range of media. Installation
art has come to encompass other terms such as 'intervention',
'interaction', 'interior art', 'ambient', 'event' and 'project'. Within the
field of Installation, such terms have equal standing and may even be
interchangeable. They are used by artists, curators and critics to further
define specific activities. The practice of Installation, then, is increasingly
characterized by its multifariousness and polyphony. Some voices have
been raised announcing the demise of Installation, or at least the
possibility of it splitting into, or being replaced by, one or other of
the terms mentioned above, though, crucially, Installation is seen
to be moving from a position of homogeneity to one that stresses its
heterogeneous nature. The process, execution and display of works now
demonstrates a variety of emphases, each informed by a different context
or enquiry. Faced with these changeable manifestations, the British artist
Keith Tyson, the Turner Prize winner in 2002, suggests that the encounter
with a work of contemporary art should not make the viewer ask 'what is
it about, but how do I feel?' Tyson asserts the need for subjective readings
as a means of dealing with unstable realities.

One of the evolving facets of Installation was pointed out by the
Canadian art historian Johanne Lamoureux who indicated a change
in artists' attitudes towards the idea of site over a decade ago.
The relationship between a work and its location, its 'site-specificity',
was once the crucial focus for artists and audiences. Lamoureux
stated that 'Installations today are often movable pieces, not the least
ephemeral, transported from exhibition to exhibition, sometimes with
slight, timely adaptations to fit a more peculiar context.' Lamoureux
foresaw the need for installations to function as packages, to be adapted
to the needs of given exhibitions, rather than being dominated by the
demands of a non-art environment. The idea of the installation package

Carl von Weiler, *Matrix*, 1998
In this work by the British artist
Carl von Weiler, television sets were
installed in a low dark space, clinging
to the ceilings and emitting feeble
sounds and light levels from their
hanging screens. The images on the
monitors were of the artist actually
hanging upside down like a bat.

or module can also be likened to the term 'interior art', suggested by
the Dutch art historian Camiel van Winkel. Interior art is discussed as a
symptom of the loss of public art by the Dutch theorist Dieter Roelstraete
who refers to Van Winkel's term, arguing that 'the individualisation of
spatial experience (or privatisation of space) by...young artists results,
at a deeper level, in the privatisation of art *tout court*.' Roelstraete mourns
the loss of public space, a place once closely associated with culture, and
productive of stable meanings and truths. The move from exterior to
interior is typified by the rise of interior art, itself a hybrid between art,
fashionable design and lifestyle culture. Furthermore, the focus on
internal space allows artists to sidestep the demands for universality
inherent in the use of public, or external space.

Though compelling, the arguments for the return of Installation to the
protected and internal space of the gallery, do not invalidate a continuing,
often parallel connection with public locations. The American art historian
Miwon Kwon perceives a change in the fixed reading of the site whether
gallery or public space. In her influential book *One Place After Another* she
calls this move away from a fixed reading 'site oriented', suggesting that
place is not about fixity, nor the extraction of a definite meaning from a
site. Rather, the move gives rise to artists whose practice is 'nomadic,
fluid and sometimes even virtual rather than restricted to a geographical

above Bruce Gilbert, *Cross over*, 1998
The British artist Bruce Gilbert
combines digital technology and
experimental sound in his installations.
For *Cross over* he dug up the gravel in
his drive which had a depression in
it and was collecting rainwater. The
puddle was transferred to a showcase
with a soundtrack of dripping water.

below Sarah Sze, *Everything that Rises
Must Converge*, 1999
Sarah Sze uses the detritus of everyday
life, brought together into organic-like
structures which expand vertically
and fill the entire exhibition space.
These fragile, meticulously arranged
constructions are adaptable to large-
scale sites, merging space and material.

place or institution.' If the site is no longer a precondition for the work,
it follows that the content of the work is not necessarily generated by
the location. On the contrary, it is negotiated by the artist through the
dialogue engendered by the project. The context, once a marker of site,
has thus been superseded by the notion of mobility, as described by,
among others, Ilya Kabakov and the Russian theorist Boris Groys.
The current idea of art as a 'project' requires a pliable time-frame and
a flexible or portable site. The freedom to travel without boundaries does
have its problems, however. The endless international displacement of
artists is likened by the American theorist Hal Foster to the activities
of an ethnographer: 'one selects a site, enters its culture and learns its
language, conceives and presents a project, only to move to the next site
where the cycle is repeated.' The problem of the location is echoed by
the Swiss artist Thomas Hirschhorn:

> It is a provisional location, since the construction will be
> dismantled after the exhibition. But it is a location which
> is unequivocal – unequivocal because I am invited to...a city
> I don't know and whose history and inhabitants I know nothing
> about. But I come with the desire to make sculptures and show
> them to the residents and visitors of this city. And so I don't want
> to make reference to anything that has to do with the city; that
> would be pretentious.... So I selected a location which is a non-
> place, i.e. a place where people can or must go for reasons that
> have nothing to do with the geography or history of the place.

Hirschhorn correctly identified the problem of immersion in a context
provided by a location or site, and Foster's comparison between the
artist and the ethnographer was indeed recognizable in the installations
by many artists throughout the 1980s and the first half of the 1990s.
As the context of the site became the content of the work, the artist was
cast in the various roles of tourguide or archivist. This position proved to

left Olav Westphalen, *E.S.U.S.,*
Extremely Site-Unspecific Sculpture, 2000

be unenviable, since it did little to 'reveal' what was not already known.
Hirschhorn's position is by no means unique among contemporary artists.
Eschewing local habits, histories and politics has allowed artists to move
from objective knowledge to the subjective and personal. This reliance on
subjectivity impacts upon how artists perceive the exhibition context.

The writer James Meyer echoes Miwon Kwon's earlier point by
coining the term 'functional site'. This site, he argues, is 'a process,
an operation occurring between sites, a mapping of institutional and
discursive filiations and the bodies that move between them (the artist's
above all). It is an informational site, a locus of overlap of text,
photographs, and video recordings, physical places and things....
It is a temporary thing; a movement; a chain of meanings devoid of a
particular focus.' Kwon's reading of site states that 'it is now structured
(inter)textually, rather than spatially, and its model is not a map but an
itinerary, a fragmentary sequence of events and actions through spaces,
that is, a nomadic narrative whose path is articulated by the passage of
the artist.'

The creation by the German artist Olav Westphalen, *E.S.U.S.*, *Extremely Site-Unspecific Sculpture* (2000), a lunar pod-like structure, provides an ironic take on this 'nomadic' tendency. 'The *E.S.U.S.* – friendly but indifferent...acknowledges any given site and adapts to it.' The work refutes local context as 'being nostalgic, at times even picturesque', preferring mobility above the stasis caused by the overemphasis on local knowledge. The American artist Spencer Tunick uses the mobility of an idea from one place to another. The recurring motif is that of hundreds of bodies lying prone at selected locations, as in *Maine* (1997). These temporary events are then documented in photographs and video. A salient feature of these displays is that all the participants are presented entirely naked, arranged in rows, piles or waves. Tunick's human subjects vary from one location to another. As bodies are replaced by new ones, the body itself is transformed into a mere component of the artwork.

The idea of the public site has become increasingly important to 'regenerative urbanism', which seeks to reanimate post-industrial city spaces. According to the writer Suzanne Lacy, this creates an uneasy relationship between the concept of the public monument and 'new genre public art', with its emphasis on temporary installations and interventions. While the prospect of maintaining relationships with spaces beyond the gallery appears attractive to artists, the latter often seem reluctant to enter into a dialogue with the civic authorities and agencies that traditionally commission such works. However, the art historian Walter Grasskamp persists in arguing the case for public art, since it moves the emphasis from the gallery to the city. Under modernism we see an increasing trend towards an internalization, that is, a return to the physical and institutional sphere of the gallery and the museum. It may therefore be argued that, 'as cultural end sites, museums reinforced the demand for the high degree of protection which art now demanded.'

opposite Spencer Tunick, *Maine*, 1997

right Keith Wilson, *Puddle*, 1999

opposite above Rodney Graham, *The King's Part*, 1999

This position clearly privileges art of a permanent nature housed indoors over one of a temporary nature in the public sphere.

It remains to be seen whether these state-sponsored approaches to public space, disguised as sculpture projects or sculpture trails, are a significant alternative to the strictures imposed by the museum, or whether it simply moves the institution outdoors. The British artist Keith Wilson's *Puddle* (1999) provides a useful counter-argument to this reading of public art. The artist simply created a depression in a path and filled it with water, creating an artificial puddle. The work caused much debate and consternation at the time and illustrates the way in which a growing number of artists are approaching public commissions. It also serves to demonstrate that the internalization referred to by Grasskamp can also be seen as a rediscovery of the artist's and spectator's subjectivity and not simply as institutional pressure. In this instance, both models – public space and the museum – are replaced by privacy and introspection.

Subjective models of space have played an important part in the visual arts throughout the 20th century. Salient examples include Piet Mondrian's studio, Kurt Schwitters' house, Marcel Duchamp's exhibition arrangements and Brian O'Doherty's description of the 'white cube'. All of these have provided readings of spatial concepts which have been of great significance to Installation art. In each case, we find a conflation of real space with the concept of an ideal model. The German art historian Oskar Bätschmann argues that one of Installation's key characteristics is the ability to form a perceivable space, modelled or arranged towards the presence of the viewer. The above examples are then reminders of the difference between lived space and experienced, or represented space.

The King's Part (1999), a mobile installation by the Canadian artist Rodney Graham, provides a complex model for art in which the mechanism is revealed rather than the intended result. The installation

below Janet Cardiff, *The Missing Voice (Case Study B)*,1999
This work by the Canadian artist Janet Cardiff is based on a soundtrack recorded on the streets of London's East End. The work lasted for fifty minutes, tracing a route through Spitalfields and towards the City of London. Part urban guide, part fiction, part *film noir*, Cardiff's audio walk engaged the listener in a narrative which shifted through time and space. Intimate, even conspiratorial, Cardiff's work created a psychologically absorbing experience.

right Carsten Höller/Rosemarie Trockel, *Ein Haus für Schweine und Menschen* (A House for Pigs and People), 1997

opposite above Maurice van Tellingen, *Shadowman*, 1999
The Dutch artist Maurice van Tellingen creates models which include photography and video. In this work Van Tellingen uses miniature scenes in which the illusion of space is heightened by the combination of the two media. The effect makes the three-dimensional image more real and the action of the drama is rendered atmospheric and filmic as the viewer remains unaware of the plot. Van Tellingen deliberately leaves the main action outside the frame of the work, thus building tension.

presents a soundproofed box in which the audience can listen to the third flute concerto of Frederick II, King of Prussia. However, no music can be heard since the flute is not blown, the only sounds is the percussive clicks of the instrument's keys performing the work.

Ein Haus für Schweine und Menschen (A House for Pigs and People,1997), a collaboration by the artists Carsten Höller and Rosemarie Trockel, combines a minimalist building with a pigsty. The building is split in half by a glass screen, separating the audience from the animals. The architecture of the work proposes an ironic model for the genetic coexistence of animals and humans. Each of these two examples presents a particular model which questions the viewer's perception of their own presence. The viewer's sensation is heightened by the artwork's ability to propose an altered relationship between the individual and their social environment (Höller/Trockel) and the actual bodily experience through the muting of sound

(Graham). In each case the model creates artificial conditions and provides an environment separate from the external world. At the same time, it is a functioning environment which offers a parallel experience in real time.

By contrast, in architecture, models and computer-generated images serve primarily as future projections for buildings, as in the case of the designs for the new Turner Museum in Margate by the Norwegian practice Snøhetta. Only the actual building provides the user with a tangible spatial sensation. In Installation, as we have seen, the model supports a particular way of addressing the viewer's experience and ceases to be merely a tool. The Dutch artist Maurice van Tellingen maintains that the scale-model, though a traditional genre, can be a miniature installation which challenges viewers' perceptions of space. The space of the installation need not be

below Snøhetta AS, Animation for *Turner Centre, Margate, England*, 2001

above Hans Op de Beeck, *Exercising the Nowhere (2)*, 2000

opposite above Sven Påhlsson, Stills from *Sprawlville*, 2002
This computer animation examines what is at the heart of American society and culture. Through the use of computer-animated images, he reveals the connection between the 'non-place' of the suburban landscape and the Virtual Reality world. Påhlsson's use of generic architectonic models comment on a society in which virtual, electronic experience replaces the actual, physical experience.

opposite below Martin Dörbaum, *Schwimmen mit Vater, de: 'Banana Yoshimoto'* (Swimming with Father), Tsugumi 2000

below Martin Dörbaum, *Microviseur 2200/H*, 2000

entered to be perceived and enjoyed. Accordingly, the painstakingly assembled works by the Belgian artist Hans Op de Beeck and the Russian artist Alexander Brodsky operate on the principle of drawing the viewer into their reduced, yet highly effective theatrical spaces. The model offers an alternative dimension to the activity of Installation art: the viewer cannot enter it other than by virtue of the imagination, albeit by reducing their own scale. This activity of translating scale, from the large to the tiny, and vice versa, provides an invaluable insight into the nature of the viewing experience.

This experience is further challenged by the development of Virtual Reality and Mixed Reality, that is, totally or partially simulated environments. This advanced use of computer technology has brought about the simulation of sites and situations, allowing us to experience different spaces at will, and additionally has called into question our perception of what is real and what is not. The idea of the virtual model differs in many aspects from the 'real' miniature, yet both could be designated as 'heterotopias', a term associated with the French philosopher Michel Foucault. Heterotopias are 'something like counter-sites, a kind of effective enacted utopia in which the real sites, all the other real sites which can be found within the culture, are simultaneously represented, contested and inverted. Places of this kind are outside of all places, even though it may be possible to indicate their location in reality.' The Swedish artist Sven Påhlsson creates entire virtual cities, while the German artist Martin Dörbaum presents private spaces drawn from the domestic. Dörbaum's spaces are achieved without the aid of photographs. They only exist in the digital realm, rather than being modelled on the basis of photographic representations. Similarly, the British artist Paul Noble's *Unified Nobson* (2001), an animated video installation, is entirely conceived in the artist's imagination. No pretense of realism

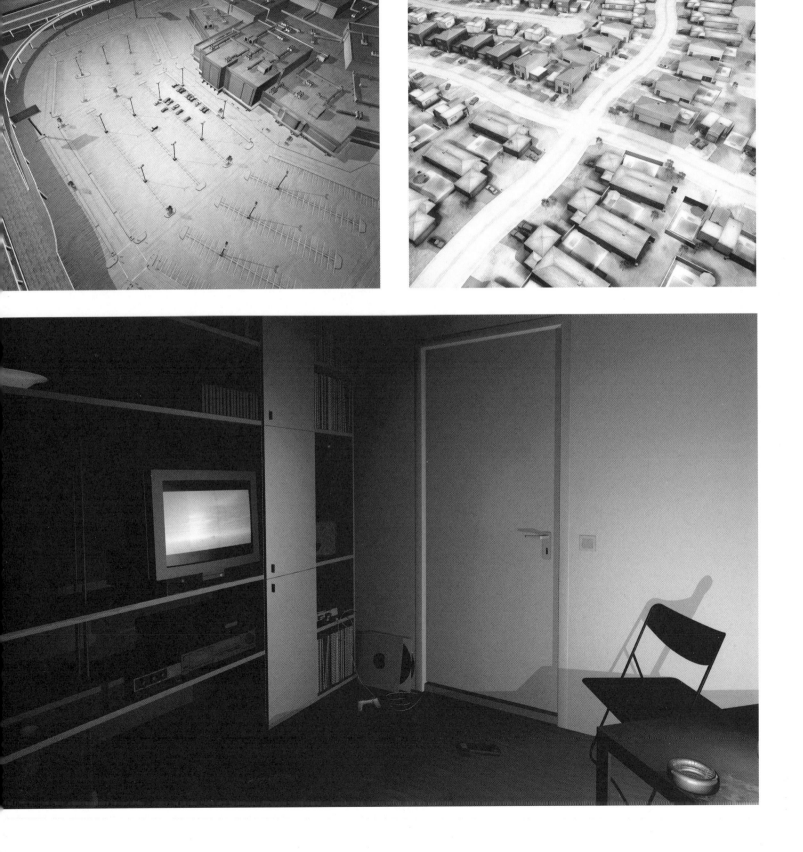

right Paul Noble, *Unified Nobson*, 2001

opposite Damían Ortega, *Cosmic Thing*, 2002
The central component of the Mexican artist Damían Ortega's work was a disassembled Volkswagen Beetle. The different car parts were suspended in the manner of a three-dimensional diagram. Beetles are still made in Puebla, Mexico, to this day, and carry notions of national identity for Mexicans, while also playing a role in the country's burgeoning globalization.

is made, and the projection reads like a black-and-white drawing, which is charming yet carries an undercurrent of menace. In his book *Being Digital*, the media theorist Nicholas Negroponte states: 'Computers and art can bring out the worst in each other when they first meet. One reason is that the signature of the machine can be too strong...the flavor of the computer can drown the subtler signals of the art.' Though technology has become an integral part of Installation art, it is the way in which artists have appropriated these advances that is important. These 'techniques' have been integrated into their work by artists, often highlighting the artificiality of the medium. Påhlsson and Dörbaum's rendering of space has nothing to do with perceived reality; on the contrary, the digital medium is exposed for what it is. The artists revel in the artificiality of their environments, pointing out that the parallel and simulated worlds of gaming are of greater interest than their real counterparts. Negroponte's

argument is thus reversed, making the centrality of the computer's signature desirable.

These spaces, like the real miniatures discussed above, might be described as simulations of elsewhere. The real site may indeed exist, but it is replaced by another version, as recalled in the painstakingly accurate scale models of the Dutch artist Frank Halmans entitled *The bedrooms in which I still wake up* (1996–2002). These installations in miniature, as the artist prefers to call them, are purported to be facsimiles of spaces in which the artist has dwelled. The intimate detail provided by the spaces (individual books on shelves, evidence of tiny hands on distressed paintwork) gives the viewer a sense of familiarity making them almost believable. Their attraction resides in the fact that the viewer is confronted with simultaneous sites: the visible simulation and its real counterpart.

The French theorist Gilles Deleuze maintains the need to reconcile these two positions: the real and the copy. He suggests that each real thing exists in different formats, including that of the simulacrum. In her book on Deleuze, the writer Claire Colebrook claims that 'each unique work of art...is a simulation.' On the basis of this statement, it might be argued that the virtual is the precondition of the real; the real, argues Deleuze, is an image first, before fulfilling its promise of becoming.

Frank Halmans, *The bedrooms in which I still wake up* (studio detail), 1996–2002

'The idea of "copy" presupposes some original model and Western thought has been dominated by the idea of the copy.' An example of this theme can be seen in Micha Ullman's installation *Empty Library* (1995) in Berlin, which marks the burning of books by Nazi students, 10 May 1933. The subterranean rectangular room filled with empty shelving can only be glimpsed through a small glass pane inserted into the cobblestones of the Bebelplatz. Here, the temporary installation has given way to a permanent monument which exhibits a 'paradoxical dysfunctionality'. The paradox resides in the fact that the installation is actually an anti-monument, it is inaccessible and difficult to view. In addition, it does not attempt to celebrate an event, preferring instead to act as a sombre

Chris Burden, *Mexican Bridge*, 1998–99
The American artist Chris Burden created a room of Meccano-like bridges, among them a model of an 19th-century bridge designed, but never built, for a gorge in Mexico and another which replicated the 1928 Tyne Bridge in Newcastle for the first round of shows at BALTIC. Standing back, the large-scale models appeared to be the same size as the Tyne Bridge which could be seen through a panoramic window.

above left Francesc Torres, *The Repository of Absent Flesh*, 1998
In this work twenty objects were displayed on separate identical steel tables in a darkened, warehouse-like space. As the viewer approached each table, a beam of light abruptly illuminated the object and a disembodied voice told the story of the display. Each one referred to a fictive character, acting as metaphors of their memory. The Catalan artist Torres created a vast archive of narrations on memory and modern identity, a portrait of our age, composed as a Proustian history.

above right Francesc Torres, *El continent de cristall* (The Crystal Continent), 1993–94
This monumental work combines a vast field of 48,000 glass bottles with a steamroller apparently making its way towards a glass house at the opposite end of the space. The installation refers to the fragility of civilization in the face of social history and political power.

warning. Ullman's installation provides a model of a library, but not of any particular one, thus eschewing the quest for authenticity.

As new forms of Installation move into the mainstream, questions of value are inevitably raised and addressed. Museums, commercial galleries and collectors have been instrumental in this change. Since more Installation art has found its way into large-scale exhibitions and, subsequently, into major collections, the relationship between the artist, the curator and the collector has been altered. While questioning exhibition practices, Installation has been central in changing the display and collection activity of institutions. The Swedish curator Maria Lind states, 'It is about scepticism and enthusiasm, affirmation and critique all at the same time. As the older generation, so to speak, "broke the ice" with their confrontations and polemics it is easier today to be more nuanced, smart and sensitive.' Installation art now combines a flexible approach to display, while insisting on interaction and discussion with the audience as an integral part of the work itself. Though the collection 'remains the key to the museum', according to the curator Hans-Ulrich Obrist, the question arises about its nature and contents. Obrist makes the distinction between objects and 'life-works'. The latter term refers to artworks involving installations, events and actions in a close relationship with the viewer. Although objects provide the backbone of the institution, it is arguable that new forms will continue to be added to collections which challenge the format and direction of the museum. These new forms may be seen as positively disruptive influences operating within the body of the collection, undermining the educational status of the museum, a development that the British writer Richard Sennett sees as beneficial. He also offers a note of caution, suggesting that participation should not

below Steven Pippin, *Addendum*, 1994 The gallery picture project of the British artist Steven Pippin is made by dividing the space so that one half acts as a camera, recording the other half as its subject. The artist's preoccupation with turning spaces into photo machines, e.g. laundromats converted into pinhole cameras, explores the issue of the self-sufficient machine, which loses its former function and takes on a personality of alienation.

opposite page Monica Bonvicini, *Plastered*, 1998
The Italian artist Monica Bonvicini opposes uncompromising and aggressive actions with the expected reverential behaviour inside the whitewashed gallery. The artist herself can be seen kicking holes in walls or demolishing spaces. In this piece the audience was invited to walk on a fragile plaster surface which covered the entire gallery floor. In one single action, the spectators destroyed the artist's work, while also disrupting the perfection of the gallery space.

substitute for interpretation, leading to the collapse of critical thinking. However, the establishment of new types of audience interaction proposes a different form of interpretation. Interaction is then not simply an opportunity to ensure the audience's participation, but instead suggests a creative engagement with the content of the artwork which directly impacts on the evaluation of the museum itself.

These developments and discussions are well under way in many contemporary institutions and have introduced new forms of display. A curious example of these changes can be found in an unlikely setting: the One Picture Gallery in Penza, Russia, can be seen as an institution unwittingly dedicated to the techniques of Installation art. Paradoxically,

it shows no installation whatsoever, instead displaying a single painting at a time. Before viewing the painting, the visitors are given a slide-show that contextualizes the work. Finally, the curtain is drawn back to reveal the single painting. The artwork is framed by a theatrical set. In this instance the experience of the work is mediated by the addition of a further frame, the frame of the proscenium arch. This setting points to the problem of attention commonly experienced in museums, as we are distracted by too many works on display. Though showing only single paintings, the museum makes use of the techniques of Installation in creating a setting for the work, thus turning the work into an environment.

In a discussion between the critics Jeffrey Kastner and Mary Jane Jacob, we are made aware of a paradigmatic shift which has taken place in the art of recent years, suggesting that 'less emphasis was placed on creating an artifact in the traditional sense, and more on exposing and challenging the processes that create cultural activity, whether or not they create art as an object.' According to Kastner's and Jacob's argument, the creation of objects becomes optional. The nomadic artist leaves no physical trace behind and simply moves on. It is arguable that Installation art, with its shift in emphasis from site to open-ended projects, leads to a 'belonging-in-transience' for artists, a state that is neither dependent on lasting objects nor on fixed locations. Accordingly, Michael Landy's installation proposes the wholesale removal of the object: the destruction of the belongings that make up the artist's material life presents a vast installation as a process culminating in dust. *Break Down* suggests a last futile stand of the idea of the *Gesamtkunstwerk*, the 'total artwork'. By confronting us with our own conspicuous consumption, Landy suggests that after art's demise there is always shopping. As Landy writes, 'This project is a kind of luxury in one respect. I don't want the work to be seen as purely negative, as a sacrifice. In a sense, it's the ultimate consumer choice.'

opposite page staatsbankberlin, *Einstein on the Beach*, 2002
For this opera/installation at the staatsbankberlin, artists from various fields as well as scientists were included in the cast. All installations assumed functions traditionally assigned to the theatre. Operatic action became sculptural, the installations provided content for the action, and the music interacted with the artworks and the architecture. During the performance – which lasted four and half hours – the spectator was free to move around in the various halls and levels of the building and explore it as an exhibition. The live music was heard throughout the space and video transmissions allowed for constant monitoring of what was happening in the other rooms. The performance space as a whole was considered as a zone of interaction between the operatic action and artistic and scientific 'intervention strategies'. The participating artists and scientists focused their research either on the relationship between private life and science or on the spectators' attitude towards the music.

escape

If a place can be defined as relational, historical and concerned with identity, then a space which cannot be defined as relational, or historical, or concerned with identity will be a non-place. The hypothesis advanced here is that supermodernity produces non-places.

Describing the sumptuous installations of the Norwegian artist Børre Sæthre, the critic Ina Blom uses the term 'immersive mode...a type of experience in which the subjective awareness...appears to merge with the artwork, so as to create a sensation of a new, more powerful, experience of totality.' Experience is mediated through the body: the degree to which our sensory faculties are stimulated is linked to the impact that an experience has on us. An 'immersive' work may be described as a mixture of sensory and narcissistic pleasure offered to the viewer. Sæthre's 'non-places' are part interior design and part filmset. We are cocooned in the lush experience of the work and identify with its retro-futuristic chic, recognizable from film and television. The artwork's aim to elicit sensual pleasure through sensory manipulation is significant as it mirrors developments in contemporary life; the theorist Frederic Jameson states that 'We are submerged...to the point where our postmodern bodies are bereft of spatial coordinates and practically incapable of distantiation.' Jameson uses the term 'submerged' to describe a space that leaves the individual in a state of confusion. This lack of orientation returns the audience to a reliance on sensation and subjectivity. The critic Paul Virilio suggests that perspectival geometry, in which space is ordered and stable, has given way to 'the relativity of an accidental, discontinuous and heterogeneous space'. These shifts mark important changes in the development of Installation in recent years, as sensation itself appears to have replaced the traditional art object. The 'immersive mode', referred to above, has become a key condition of viewing: it appears to indicate a withdrawal into the self, to a place of bodily sensation. It allows artists to propose an escape from perceived reality which no longer offers stable boundaries.

The Chinese writer Sze Tsung Leong suggests that the term 'space' has been superseded by the idea of 'control space'. Space, in other words, no longer exists as a three-dimensional construct, but instead 'enables the packaging of total environments – the total engagement of the senses – where sights, smells, sounds, feelings are engineered, refined... and deployed for maximum effect. Control space,' Leong continues, 'can be anywhere.' Leong's idea of space provides a useful example for the new interpretation of Installation art. The loss of 'site', discussed in the Introduction, can be linked to changes in our urban experience: the city is no longer perceived as an entity or object, nor is it based on traditional human relationships. In other words, the city is now marked by discontinuity and uncertainty, it has become a 'non-place'. The way we think about space is therefore wholly experiential and is reliant on a series of stimuli, which renders our perception of it much more fluid and transient.

The American artist Andrea Zittel's installation *Raugh Furniture: Lucinda* (1998) provides an ironic look at how we inhabit public and private space. It is a living-room setting in which nature merges with the man-made environment. The gallery in which the installation is presented is occupied by large rock formations of foam rubber, which double as seating and sleeping arrangements. The outside, usually unforgiving and hard, is transformed into a comfortable and relaxing interior fit for human enjoyment. The same artist's *A–Z Escape Vehicles* (1996), designed like minimalist survival capsules, extend the artist's concern with containment and comfort. While their very mobility alludes to and elicits a sense of nomadism, the displacement also acknowledges a desire for solitude, for withdrawal into the self.

The themes of privacy and contemplative withdrawal are echoed in the works of artists such as Gregor Schneider, Lee Bul and Absalon. Absalon, from Israel, foresaw the audience's fascination with intimate spaces in the early 1990s. His installations,

each carrying the title *Cellule* (1991–92), took the form of white cardboard and plaster structures, tailor-made for the artist. These minimal cells displayed a monastic quality which lent itself to contemplation. 'By modifying the architecture, I compelled the visitors to be aware of themselves inside my space,' says Absalon. 'Thus, through his vision of a few items meant for his own use and adapted for rest and peace of mind, the artist describes the domestic universe.' By contrast, the Korean artist Lee Bul presents shiny plastic shells which are highly engineered. Rather than inspired by architecture, they are derived from cutting-edge product design. The futuristic pods, cocoon the individual within environments made for single persons.

If the audience in the work of Absalon and Bul is reduced to the individual, it could be argued that the German artist Gregor Schneider requires no public at all. His work *The Dead House Ur*, (1985–) often related to Kurt Schwitters's celebrated *Merzbau*, consists of the endless remodellings of his house in his native town of Rheydt. The work is 'solitary and secretive' and involves covering the interior with a separate layer by copying or doubling what is beneath. The actual work receives few visitors, but, occasionally, Schneider rebuilds sections of it in museums and galleries. His *Ur* appears to be a celebration and excavation of a specific site, yet on closer examination it is revealed to be a simulation, a situation in which all semblance of the original is lost. As states the

French theorist Jean Baudrillard, 'It is no longer a question of imitation, nor duplication, nor even parody. It is a question of substituting the signs of the real for the real.' The house, its history and function are obliterated by the installation which mimics the original. Although ostensibly the same, the artwork shares none of the house's characteristics and functions, leading to a clear separation between what is real and what is not. The French writer Bernard Marcadé writes of a certain utopia that is 'situated in the non-place of the world'. These are 'locations which of themselves constitute universes provided with an autonomous economy and an autonomous imaginary realm'. Marcadé's notion of a 'non-place' utopia might be shared by the Swiss artists Biefer/Zgraggen, whose work entitled *God* (1998) proposes a parody of a space of worship in the shape of a vast styrofoam dome construction. Lit from within, its surface, rather than being perfectly finished, is roughly constructed in the manner of a stage set. A changing room is provided for viewers to remove their clothes before confronting *God*. The artists stated:'When you look at something beautiful, you also feel as if you are being observed by what you are observing.' The viewer is 'scrutinized' by the work and by other viewers, who themselves are also naked. Although the idea of the 'immersive' may be represented ironically in Biefer/Zgraggen's work, the notion of immersiveness indicates the broadening of references and attitudes towards space and its

relation to the spectator's body. In the Belgian artist Ann Veronica Janssen's work *Blue, Red and Yellow* (2001), steam is released into a specially constructed plexiglas space. The external walls are coated with transparent coloured film, which allows natural light to infuse the room. Unable to see the confines of the space, the audience is enveloped in dense fog which generates shifting patterns of coloured light. As the American artist and writer Robert Smithson has argued, museum and gallery spaces could thus become venues for new forms of entertainment, like 'discotheques'. Janssen's work borrows the sense of euphoria generated by the use of light and sound made in night clubs. *Blue, Red and Yellow* generates an atmosphere that is reliant on the audience's ability to 'let go' and become 'lost' in the work.

The connection between club culture and Installation is no accident. The writer Aldo Bonomi characterizes club culture as 'the quest for outer limits and the realisation of fantasies' which 'are at the heart of existential experience...a smooth space where lived time pursues a glimmering trip-hop of impulses and emotions.' The ambience in clubs is at once introspective, immersive and social; these spaces provide compelling examples of human activity which may cross over into the production and reception of art. In galleries and museums we are now witnessing the rise of a new conviviality brokered by the desire to communicate with others. This activity of spending time in the public space provided by art ranges from interaction and conversation to simply sharing the place with others, while witnessing an event, a familiar occurence for any theatre, concert or cinema-goer. The installation is therefore a focal point for the viewer's attention, as well as a meeting place.

The work of the American artist Doug Aitken exemplifies the change in audience's expectation and attitude. In his exhibition 'New Ocean', at the Serpentine Gallery in London (2002), he showed a wide range of large-scale video projections. The interior of the gallery was remodelled to house 360-degree projections of waterfalls, melting glaciers and other natural phenomena. Eschewing the usual formality of the gallery, the audience was invited to sit or lie on the floor in the darkened rooms to enjoy the spectacle. The work created a viewing environment that was part cinematic and part 'chill-out lounge'. Works such as New Ocean are indicative of certain types of installations as 'ambients', relaxed spaces that envelop the viewer while stimulating their senses. Such places are not unique to Installation art, however, and find their counterparts in design and music developments, as well as in 'lifestyle culture'. Other examples of this tendency are found in work by the American partnership Diller+Scofidio whose media pavilion for Swiss Expo 2002 entitled Blur Building (2002) – a platform rising from a lake, and shrouded in an artificial cloud – promotes a harmonic relationship between the architectural space, the surrounding landscape and the audience. Viewers are cocooned in high-tech rainmacs which keep them dry as they negotiate the pavilion, and eventually end up in a bar. Diller+Scofidio made use of extensive sensory stimuli to immerse their audiences in environments that fostered sociability through shared experience.

A different approach to immersivity was given in the collaboration of the British artists Bruce Gilchrist and Jo Joelson entitled Polaria (2002), the result of a research project in Greenland. On site, over several weeks, the artists recorded natural light conditions. The final work consisted of a white booth with a perspex ceiling which hid an arsenal of fluorescent lights. Viewers entered the space one at a time wearing an insulated white coat and sat in a clear perspex chair. By resting their hands on copper transmitters in the armrests of the chair, the electrical circuit was closed. The lights overhead came on and their luminosity could be controlled by the amount of pressure exerted on the copper pads. The experience of the arctic light was enhanced by the low ambient temperature in the booth. Although the installation referred to a specific site in the sub-polar region, the white booth at its centre merely proposed a space that enveloped the spectator, allowing the individual to explore the changing light conditions. Greenland thus ceased to be a real site and was replaced by the spectator's imagination. The roots of works such as Polaria are arguably to be found in the 'sites' and 'non-sites' of Minimal artists of the 1960s, which traced the relationship between

Marcel Biefer/ Beat Zgraggen
God, 1998

outdoor and gallery spaces as a means of critiquing 'display'; yet a crucial change in current artists' attitudes has emerged: no critique of the exhibition system is intended, instead, the focus rests with the viewer as a sentient being.

The immersive space remains fundamentally an experiential and sentient place, though it is also a means of escaping our everyday conditions. Often departing from the artist's body, needs and imagination it succeeds in disconnecting the spectators from their everyday surroundings and transporting them to a place of contemplation. This is not a direct contemplation of the world first and foremost, but a viewing of the self contemplating the external world. As Franz Kafka wrote:'It seems to me that I am not in front of my house, but in front of myself, in front of myself sleeping, and that I at the same time have the joy of sleeping profoundly and of guarding over myself as a sentry.'

Per Barclay

right *Pas de deux*, 2001
In this work two chainsaws 'performed' a violent dance, choreographed to the sound of the destruction of the space. The human figure was physically absent, but potentially threatened. The Norwegian artist creates spaces of palpable tension. He confronts the viewer with the absence of comfort, pointing out issues of sublime and 'terrible' beauty.

below *Untitled*, 1999–2000
This installation by the Norwegian artist consisted of two inflatable structures of parachute silk, powered by motorized fans. The envelopes changed form as the supply of air varied, resembling a giant organism. While gently billowing, the structures were nonetheless perceived as invasive and suggestive of coerciveness. Though the audience perceived no threat, its freedom of movement became restricted.

above and left Lee Bul, *Gravity Greater Than Velocity II*, 1999

The work of the Korean artist Lee Bul consisted of three 'karaoke pods', installed with a video and corresponding song list which addressed a specific theme. In the privacy of the soundproofed, highly designed car-pods the viewer was provided with an opportunity to indulge in a solo performance. The work referred to the significance of karaoke in contemporary Asian cultures.

Bul's work also includes funky street performances, outlandish installations and interactive sculptures. Monstrous and grotesque goddesses are mixed with science-fiction manga characters which interact with cyborgs and sexually predatory living dolls.

above Ann Veronica Janssens, *Blue, Red and Yellow*, 2001
The Belgian artist Ann Veronica Janssens confronts the visitor
with an empty translucent space filled with mist. Coloured
film covers the external skin of the room. Referring to the
tradition of colour field, the artist confronts the beholder
with an immersive non-site without boundaries.

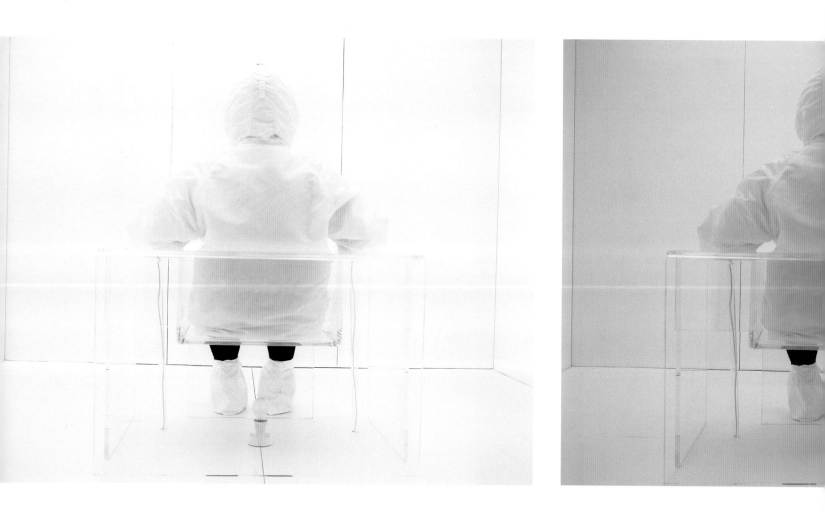

below Bruce Gilchrist and Jo Joelson, *Polaria*, 2002
Returning from their research trip in Greenland, the British artists Bruce Gilchrist and Jo Joelson created a simulated daylight chamber. One visitor at a time, wearing a white overall, entered the immersive chamber. By placing their hands on two copper plates the audience triggered virtual daylight responses. The chamber makes explicit the nature of the body as a technology in itself. The body is both the source of the data and its receptor, both recorder and transmitter of phenomena.

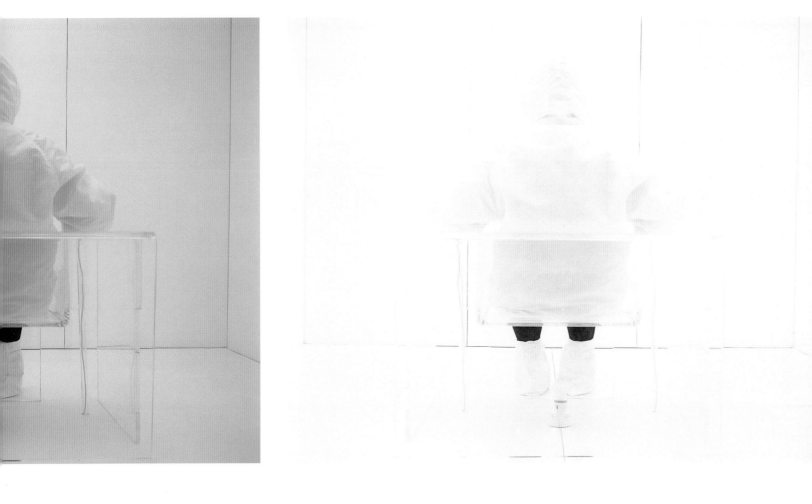

below Jaume Plensa, *Love Sounds I-V*, 1998
The viewer opened a small metal door to enter each of the five cubicles made of alabaster bricks and illuminated from within. Once inside, the isolated viewer heard amplified sounds, which were recordings of five different points on Plensa's body. The Spanish artist recorded the fluid passing through his body, creating an inner world of sounds normally inaccessible to our perception.

opposite page Ernesto Neto, *Walking in Venus blue cave*, 2001
Ernesto Neto creates worlds between the body and architecture. His work articulates the spaces of buildings while simulating bodily membranes. These structures are constructed from polyamide, shaped by being pulled across architectural spaces or gorged with substances like powdered turmeric or lead shot. The process is always intrinsic to the form. Neto has created entire rooms out of polyamide material suspended from existing ceiling structures. The corners are weighted and looped over beams or rings to create a semitransparent cube with concave walls. These walls are disturbingly skin-like, an association that the artist sometimes highlights by embroidering small orifices into the membrane. Other polyamide objects are arranged in clusters, taking the form of soft standing tubes, like fungi or crowds of amorphous figures. In every case the works are highly sensual, an experience heightened by the aroma of turmeric or cloves, which strikes visitors long before they see the installations.

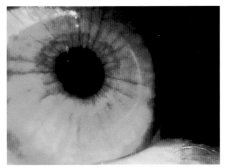

above Pipilotti Rist, *Sip My Ocean (Grossmut Begatte Mich)*, video still, 1994–96
The Swiss Video artist Pipilotti Rist understands the impact of pop culture on audiences and she has appropriated the style of music videos with their fast pace and message-induced content. *Sip My Ocean* provides an example of this with its music track and ambient mood.

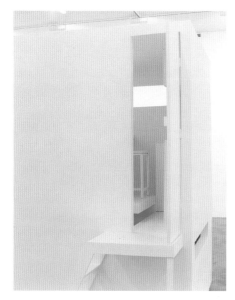

left (above and below) Absalon, *Cellule nr.6*, 1992
The Israeli-born artist Absalon made a series of works entitled *Cellules*. These were mock-ups of architectonic spaces he planned to install in major cities around the world. They were intended to be his home, like stations in a nomadic life. Based on combinations of the square and the circle, every *Cellule* was self-contained and painted pristine white. Combining elements from the ideals of Le Corbusier with the rigours of the Bauhaus, he produced models of mental and physical spaces. The interiors were cramped, the proportions of the spaces exclusively fitted the artist's body.

opposite above Børre Sæthre, *MY PRIVATE SKY, unit1/trauma white*, 2001
The spatial creations of the Norwegian artist Børre Sæthre focus on our permanent and innate desires for comfort, relaxation and luxury. His artificial, aesthetically perfect environments, echo retro or futuristic filmsets, as might be found in style magazines. Though appealing seductively to voyeuristic and narcissistic needs, the interiors of the artist leave the viewer powerless and isolated. Sæthre's work simulates the experience of a fake totality, trapping the viewer in the construction of a virtual reality environment.

right Siobhan Hapaska, *Here*, 1995
The Irish artist's work was exhibited at Documenta 9 in 1995. The visitor lay on a sheepskin-covered bed, inhaling oxygen from a cylinder to the sound of water trickling all around. The work had a futuristic feel, luxurious and seductive. Hapaska creates works that evoke feelings of escape and travel. This piece also contained sound, fragmented narratives oscillating between hyper-reality and evocations of strange road movies.

right Gregor Schneider,
Ur12 Total isoliertes Gästezimmer
(Completely Insulated Guest Room)
Rheydt, 1995
For the German artist Gregor Schneider
the house acts as a mirror, a thin barrier
between the world as it is, and the world
as he would like it to be. In Schneider's
terms the house is a space of reclusion,
a shrine for anxieties, needs and
aspirations. In the late 1980s the artist
started transforming his house into a
projection of his thoughts. Constantly
assembling, excavating, constructing
and deconstructing, he has rebuilt
walls, added rooms, corridors and
wells, turning his house into a labyrinth.

The house takes on its own personality
and life, claustrophobic and silent, a
totally hermetic environment allowing
the artist to act out, unseen, his
imagined desires and fears. Schneider
reconstructs the house from the
original as a series of public
installations. He meticulously takes
apart the original and reassembles
parts in public museums and galleries.
The overall game of reconstruction,
display of the real, or fake, fuses
together into a blind Borgian play
with no beginning or end.

below Mischa Kuball, *'Believe/ Disbelieve'*, 1999
Kuball's installation focused on blurring the boundaries of built space. Two large motorized mirror-balls spun in the space, while projectors beamed slides with letters from the alphabet onto their surfaces. The room, lit by moving specks of light, appeared to be spinning simultaneously in two opposed directions, producing an effect which was both vertiginous and unnerving.

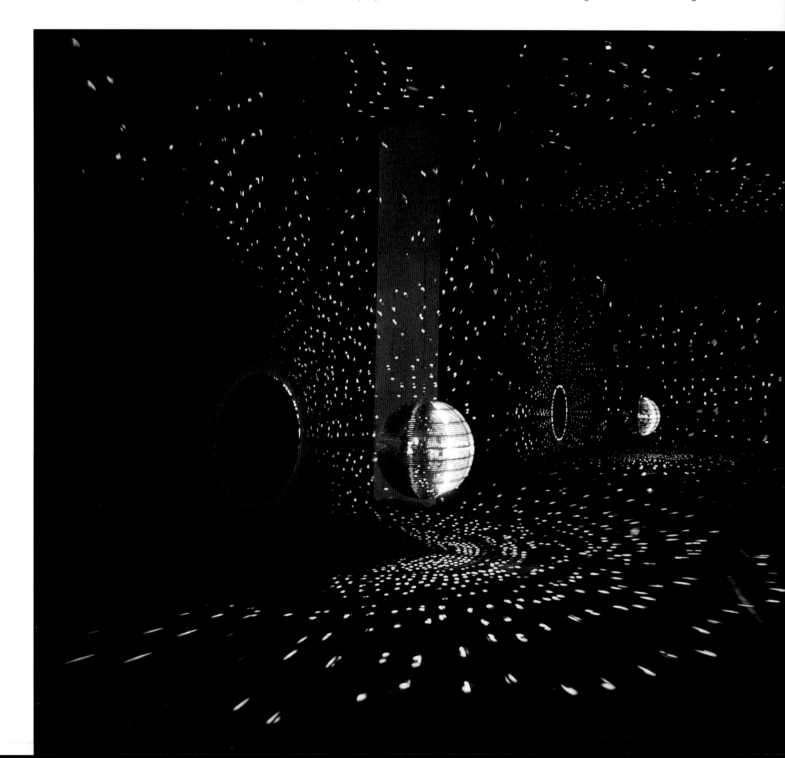

below right Kazuo Katase, *Winterreise*, 1998
The installation of the Japanese artist Kazuo Katase made use of elementary geometries and the play of light and shadow. It was built around the Zen concept of *koan-chaos-satori*, meaning 'the way', a term associated with Japanese sites and ritual. He extends this theme to other situations, through contemplation of Western philosophies and an involvement with theatrical elements – stage sets and spatial dramatization. His work points out that the meaning of being cannot be grasped rationally, only experienced.

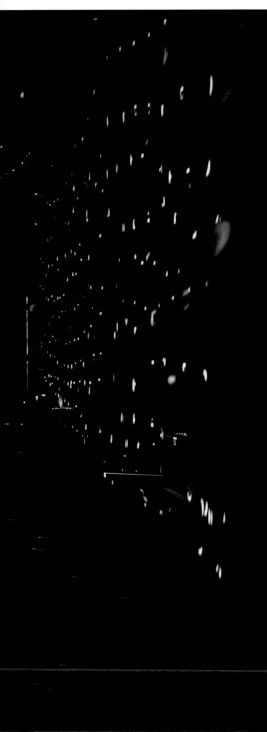

opposite above Pierre Huyghe, *L'expédition scintillante, a musical, Act 1, Act 2, Act 3* (The Glistening Expedition) 2002
The French artist Pierre Huyghe set up an imaginary journey to Antarctica as a musical, using spatial stagings which included ice, water, rain, fog and snow. A large ship made of ice slowly melted in one of the galleries, while elsewhere a black skating rink served as the stage for the musical. The entire building was programmed so that light, weather, music and action followed a filmscript.

opposite below Yayoi Kusama, *Dots Obsession*, 2000
This work was presented at the Consortium in Dijon in 2000. Fifty years of involvement in contemporary art has established her as a phenomenon. Her work, as she describes it, is a reflection of her inner life; it includes poetry, novel writing, sculpture and painting and constitutes a body without limits or boundaries. She has taken up residence in a psychiatric hospital where the calm and solitude allow her dreams to travel.

right (above and below)
Jon Lockhart and Tom Cox-Bisham, *Jon Thomas: Together in Electric Dreams*, 2002
The British artists John Lockhart and Tom Cox-Bisham's work entirely transformed the exhibition space, covering every surface with pink and white vinyl, producing a mock-minimal 1980s look. Blue grids covered the white surfaces, alluding to the banal computer aesthetic of the minor classic film *Tron* (1981), in which the hero is imprisoned in a virtual space. Semitransparent plastic sheeting covering the walls hid endless banks of old audio appliances of which the operating lights flickered and flashed intermittently. The movement and sound generated in each space was monitored via microphones which gave an overall atmosphere of claustrophobia and entrapment. The installation gave the participators total sensory overload as if they were physically immersed in the computer game. Finally, they were offered an exit through a false escape hatch smelling of cherries.

above Julian Opie, *Imagine that you are moving*, 1997
This work was installed at Terminal 1, Heathrow Airport in 1997. In a secure enclosure, designed by the architect Richard Rogers to cater specifically for transit passengers making connections with international flights, Opie's commission presented a stylized vision of the British landscape on four massive lightboxes which ran the full length of the atria and dominating the whole space. This encounter with Britain was inverted in the second part of Opie's work; dispersed around the transfer lounge waiting area were a series of closed circuit monitors. These showed the same stylized landscape, but the images travelled across the screens. The viewer was static but the landscape moved on.

left and below Ugo Rondinone,
*It's late and the wind carries a faint sound
as it moves...*, 1999/2000
Inside a room flooded in blue light,
six large-format, black-and-white video
projections with twelve loops showed
women and men performing simple
acts – walking, lying down, dancing.
Using atmospheric material from retro
feature films combined with his own
film material and a soundtrack, the
Swiss artist Ugo Rondinone created
a performative situation of sustained
action and enclosed space.

below Doug Aitken, *Thaw*, 2001
During the exhibition 'New Ocean' by the American artist
Doug Aitken, the viewer entered the exhibiting space through
the basement, descending into the darkness of its utility
spaces and resurfacing in the central body of the Serpentine
Gallery's dome. The overall effect of the work gave the feeling
of being submerged, like swimming in a weightless space.
Surrounded by projections and swallowed by the play of
shadows and colour, the disoriented viewer tried to find
their own intimate order in this apparently fragmented vision.
Literal space was transformed into psychological space.

opposite far right Dalziel+Scullion, *Rain*, 2000
The structure of this work by Scottish artists Dalziel+Scullion
was conceived as a temporary pavilion for the contemplation
of rain. A tin roof amplified the sound of rain, and channelled
it into a collecting pool at the rear. The pavilion was entered by
a long wooden ramp, and a bench was provided for visitors.
The walls of the structure were clad in a cellular plastic
material, which reflected light during the daylight hours.
In the evening the structure was lit by an animated 'gobo'
system which created a stylized pattern of rain on the walls.

opposite above left Ann Lislegaard,
I-You-Later-There, 2000
The Danish artist Ann Lislegaard's
work challenged the viewer's
sensory perceptions. Her use of
logical connections of sight and sound
were contrasted with aggressive shifts
between light and dark.

opposite below Ron Haselden,
Maid of The Mist, 1994
The British artist Ron Haselden divided
the exhibition space into two parts
through a large white screen suspended
at a 45-degree angle across the space.
Two projections using a theatrical
device projecting fire and clouds
alternated on either side of the screen.
Live sounds were relayed from different
areas inside and outside the space.

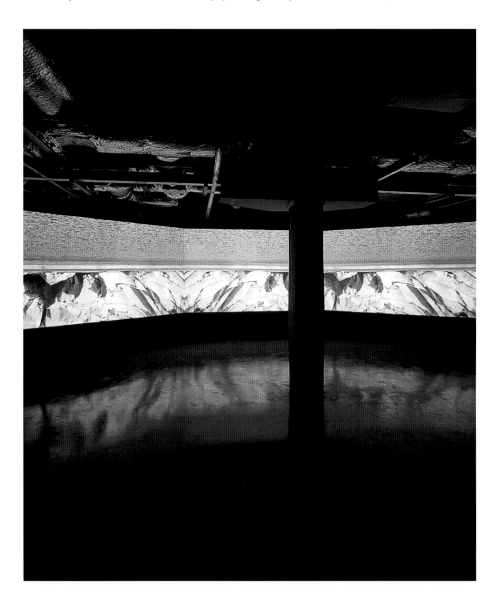

Diller+Scofidio, *Blur Building*, 2002
Diller+Scofidio is a collaborative, interdisciplinary studio which fuses architecture, visual and performing arts. The team is primarily involved in thematically driven experimental work which takes the form of temporary and permanent site-specific installations, multimedia theatre, electronic media, and publishing.

Blur Building, a media pavilion created for the Swiss Expo 2002, was situated at the base of Lake Neuchâtel in Yverdon-les-Bains, Switzerland. A fine mist sprayed through thirteen thousand nozzles created an artificial cloud 300 feet wide (91 m), 200 feet deep (70 m) and 65 feet high (20 m). A built-in weather station controlled the fog output by responding to the shifting climatic conditions, measuring the temperature, humidity, wind direction and wind speed. The public approached the *Blur* via a bridge. The 400-foot long (122 m) ramp deposited visitors at the centre of the fog mass on a large open-air platform. Visual and acoustic references were erased when entering the fog, leaving only an optical 'white-out' and 'white noise' of pulsing water nozzles. Entering the cloud, each visitor was asked to respond to a

questionnaire and received a 'braincoat' (smart raincoat). The coat was used as protection from the wet and for storing the personality data of the audience communicating with the cloud's computer network. Using tracking and location technology, the position of each visitor could be identified, and as they passed one another, the coats compared profiles and changed colour indicating the degree of attraction or repulsion, much like an involuntary blush. The system allowed interaction among four hundred visitors at a time. Visitors could climb another level to the Angel Bar at the summit. The final ascent resembled the sensation of flight as visitors pierced through the cloud layer to the open sky.

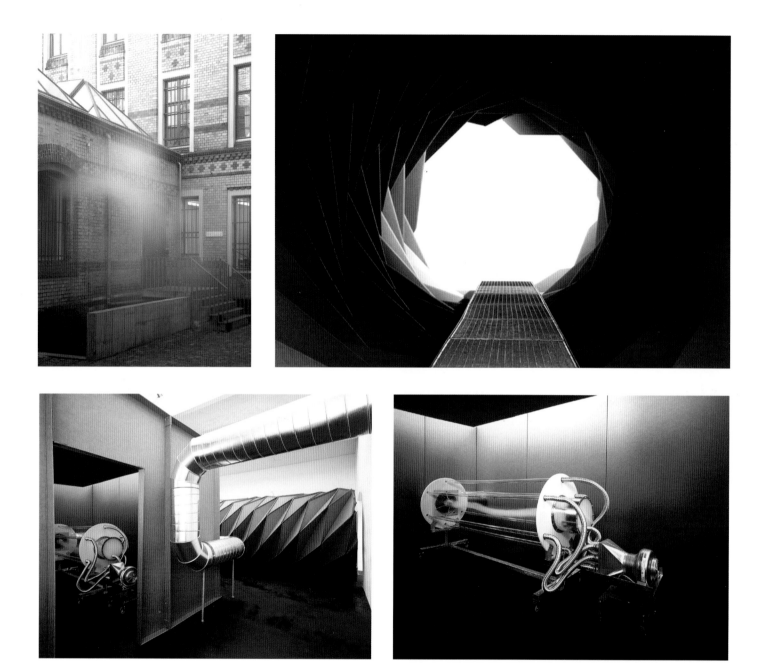

this page and opposite above Olafur Eliasson, *Die Dinge die du nicht siehst* (The Things You Cannot See), 2001.
The Danish artist Olafur Eliasson is primarily interested in a simulation of natural phenomena as art, while at the same time revealing the technique used to recreate it. His ultimate aim is to question our very perception of reality. The entrance to the exhibition was turned into a cardboard tunnel. When visitors walked through it, an optical illusion occurred which made it appear to rotate on its own axis. A machine produced a fog spiral in a side space that contorted and changed shape as the visitors progressed down the tunnel. The fog was expelled into the courtyard where, according to atmospheric conditions, it became more, or less, visible.

left Louise Sudell, *Ascensor Negro* (Black Lift), 1998

The British artist Louise Sudell often uses magic tricks and entrapment in her installations. In this work she was influenced by the famous escapologist, Harry Houdini. When spectators inside the lift pressed a button to open the door, instead they became trapped inside. At the same time a video link was activated so that viewers outside could see the panic on the faces of the people inside. Sudell is well aware of the potential for control which exists in the relationship between the artist and the viewer.

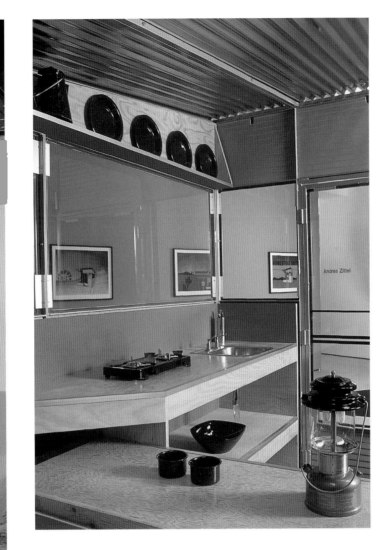

below Carl von Weiler, *Nest*, 1993–96
The installation by the London-based artist was a long-term project involving the excavation of earth from the disused basement of a London studio complex. Out of a journey governed by hand digging and exchanging earth for wooden planking, a subterranean 'container' comprising two rooms at different levels and a long connecting corridor began to emerge. The climate was regulated according to body temperature using small heaters and a cooling fan.

Andrea Zittel
above *A–Z Homestead Unit*, 2001
left *Raugh Furniture: Lucinda*, 1998
Though the American artist Andrea Zittel's chairs do not actually provide the most comfortable position for the body. *Raugh Furniture*, inspired by the habits of a dog, which daily changed its resting places, is a form of environmental furniture which can be carved or sculpted continuously as the need in the space changes. This attempt to discover new ways in which to position the body both spatially and socially focuses on Zittel's preoccupation with the nomadic state of human beings. *A–Z Homestead Unit* plays on the concept of ideal spaces for contemporary living, which cater for individuals' needs.

above Lee Bul, *Live Forever*, 2001
This futuristic installation involved video projection and three soundproofed karaoke booths, pod-like capsules in which visitors could give a solo performance. Bul first created a karaoke booth for *Gravity Greater Than Velocity II*. The pods in *Live Forever* continued the artist's exploration of the significance of karaoke in contemporary Asian culture.

Doug Aitken
left *Blow Debris*, 2000
This video installation depicts the lives of people living in a deserted landscape (the Mojave Desert, Salton). They appear as nomadic squatters moving restlessly in a post-industrial age.
below *New Skin*, 2002
Aitken's multi-screen Video installation addresses the relationships between man and his contemporary surroundings. It follows a young woman in a Tokyo apartment who is losing her sight and is consuming images for her subjective archive. The narratives reveal themselves in ambiguous windings in which the viewer is engaged: physically by passing through the space, and mentally as the images prevent a single linear viewing.

author and institution

The relationship between art and the institutions in which art is displayed, such as museums, came to play an increasingly important role in the production and reception of art from the 1960s onwards. By the early 1980s, the questioning of the relationships of power between authorship and institutions was seen by many critics as necessary for a postmodern practice, as argued by Hal Foster: '...just as the conceptual artists extended the minimalist analysis of the art object, so too...later artists have opened up the conceptual critique of the art institution in order to intervene in ideological representations and languages of everyday life.' Progressively, artists have come to resist the centrality of the institution in their work. They now tend to move away from projects displayed inside museums, even when given license to critique internal power structures, thus showing their reluctance to participate in arguments formulated by and for museum professionals.

Although artists acknowledge the importance of the gallery space as a means of disseminating their work, the idea of fusing the exhibition with the concept of the gallery has gained ground. In so doing, Installation artists are able to circumvent the agenda of the institution, albeit by appropriating its language and organizational structures. An ironic example of this appropriation strategy can be seen at the Leytonstone Center for Contemporary Art. This organization, launched in 2001, is run by the British artist Bob & Roberta Smith and the American artist and curator Jessica Voorsanger. Leytonstone, a London suburb, houses no significant arts venues. The grandly named Center contains a single skylit exhibition space in a purpose-built shed at the end of the artist's garden. The space may be viewed as a complete artwork or as an art centre in name only, which parodies existing modes of display. It follows that the 'white cube', synonymous with the idea of display, may be removed from the museum or the gallery and reappear in the context of an artist's suburban garden. The Thai artist Navin Rawanchaikul provided an alternative to the standard gallery. His *I [love] TAXI* (2001) was an exhibition space in which the emphasis was on its reduced scale and portable nature. Artists were invited to create installations in the back of the cab for future passengers. Thus, the audience was reduced to small numbers of individuals who hailed the taxi for the purpose of transport while witnessing an art event.

Though alternative display spaces have been instrumental in the presentation of new and challenging works, their strategies have also been adopted by mainstream galleries. Michael Elmgreen and Ingar Dragset, from Denmark and Norway, install Modernist white cubes in galleries, museums and public spaces. These architectural interventions betray an ironic return to Modernist, functional design principles and simultaneously act as spaces for 'cruising', that is for sexual encounters. Their exhibit *Taking Place* (2001–2002) at the Kunsthalle in Zurich, on the other hand, literally tore down the walls of the galleries, disrupting the workings of the institution. Nothing was completed, rather, it was the upheaval generated by destruction and rebuilding that constituted the work. Elmgreen & Dragset's installation echoed the ideas of the architect and urbanist Cedric Price who proposed that buildings should not be long-lasting, but should disintegrate after a few years. Price also argued that the 21st-century museum should use uncertainty and incompleteness as a catalyst for change.

However, according to Maria Lind, curator at the Moderna Museet in Stockholm, the museum continues to be 'thought of as a place of display, a showroom, and exhibitions are taken for granted as the natural way of dealing with art.' Lind goes on to describe a type of work that 'is oriented towards the everyday. It generally wants to avoid the solemnity and the static quality that often embody institutions, when it is not downright critical of them.' Lind argues that the institution is not dismissed or rejected by these projects, but is 'problematised'. The Swiss-born curator Hans Ulrich Obrist has suggested a shift in the culture of museums, to transform them into 'laboratories'. He states that 'the idea of embracing contradictions is very important.... The laboratory is

about leaving the museum, is against the museum.' Obrist is known for innovative exhibitions and concepts which have travelled to cities worldwide. These include *Cities on the Move* (with the Chinese curator Hou Hanru) in London, Bordeaux, Humblebæk, Helsinki, Vienna and Bangkok (1997–99), *Unbuilt Roads* (1997) with Guy Tortosa and *Do It* (1994–2001), an exhibition format presented in numerous different cities. Obrist advocates flexible exchange with artists, curators and architects. Influenced by Obrist's working methodology, a group of 105 artists, working under the rubric *Morphing Systems* took over a former hospital in Zurich (1998) and began to intervene and interact with each other's works over a period of six months. The hospital site provided in the first place a point of reference for the artists, only to be replaced as the focus for subsequent interventions.

It remains significant that these projects are always accompanied by a publication. Once simply described as 'exhibition catalogues' which complemented the exhibitions, these publications have come to alter, add to, and indeed challenge the perception of the work. The photograph, as a means of documenting a work of art, has had an important role in preserving temporary installations. Indeed, it might be argued that the photograph (in books, magazines and on the internet) has become a major means of viewing Installation art, and that it has superseded witnessing the actual work in situ. Walter Benjamin and André Malraux wrote extensively about the photograph's power to change our perception of art. The result of this technique of reproduction was a waning of uniqueness. While Installation art, through its temporal nature and reliance on place, does not require uniqueness per se, it nonetheless depends on the viewer's experience. The photograph may serve as an aide-mémoire, but it can only offer a view, without transmitting the experience of the work. The display of an installation via a photograph certainly alters its reception as we move from the position of the viewer to that of the reader or browser.

The art theorist Brian O'Doherty refers to the perception of the viewer by stating: 'Avant-garde gestures have two audiences: one which was there and one – most of us – which wasn't.' O'Doherty goes on to argue that the original audience completes the work through memory after seeing the work. 'We from a distance know better. The photographs of the event restore to us the original moment, but with much ambiguity.' Ilya Kabakov, who arguably wrote the most detailed 'manual' in existence for Installation art, argues that 'any installation is incredibly, impossibly sensitive to the place where it is constructed.' To Kabakov, firsthand experience of the work remains crucial. Although we have become used to the documentary value of the photograph (and video) in communicating installations to wider audiences, rarely do we question how our experience is altered by the shift from presence to reproduction. By placing the work in the context of a publication, the viewer's perception of the work is irrevocably altered. The publication is not simply a means of extending the exhibition's visibility, but it allows curators, artists and designers to rework the context in which the work is shown. This has resulted in innovative ways of displaying installation projects, while allowing the artistic and curatorial processes involved in the work to become revealed. Salient published examples include Rem Koolhaas/Hans Ulrich Obrist's *Mutations* (2001), *Morphing Systems'* eponymous catalogue, Damien Hirst's *I want to spend the rest of my life everywhere, with everyone, one to one, always, forever, now* (1997). The key difference between the traditional catalogue and these examples, is that the more innovative publication extends the possibilities for dialogue and the remit of the installation itself. The publication has thus replaced the importance of site to become the place and meaning of the work. Countless catalogues and magazines have aspired to present 'exhibitions' on the printed page, as predicted by Malraux, in his *Musée Imaginaire*: 'A museum without walls has been opened to us, and it will carry infinitely farther that limited revelation of the world of art which the real museums offer us within their walls: in answer to their appeal the plastic arts have produced their printing press.'

The 're-presentation' of Installation art through a range of different formats confirms its position as a versatile and even unpredictable activity. In his book

From Subject to Project (1994), the Czech cultural critic Vilém Flusser suggested that the notion of the 'project' defined our identity, as it is engagement in some activity that gives us our place in the world. Similarly, installations have come to be increasingly referred to as 'projects', suggesting a greater emphasis on a work's process, while keeping the production of a work more flexible and open-ended as well as stressing its collaborative nature. Such works now require a range of skills, significant financial input and negotiations to secure a location. Thus the project begins as a collaboration, that is to say that 'interaction' is built into the work from the very start. Funding agencies and institutions need to be secured from the outset, rather than solicited later on out of necessity. Such partnerships are not without their problems and they do impact on the work. As Kasper König, director of the Museum Ludwig in Frankfurt suggests: 'The art museum can act as a producer concerning contemporary art...I think this is an important task.' On the other hand, Jerôme Sans, co-curator of the Palais de Tokyo in Paris, continues to question whether the 'museum is really a place for experimentation'. Sans's position is echoed by a growing number of innovative arts organizations which attempt to elude the grasp of the institution. Locus+, founded in 1993, is an organization with networks of artistic centres in the UK and Canada. Its commissioning policy is centred on the artist instead of the institution, 'thus opposing the norm accepted on the UK art scene,' writes Àgnes Ivacs. While artists struggle for acknowledgment of their authorial credentials, institutions have moved away from being solely collectors to being also producers of new works. However, conflicts of ownership may arise between artists and commissioning institutions. 'The work is indivisible from the persona of the artist,' argues Miwon Kwon, 'the intricate orchestration of literal and discursive sites that make up a nomadic narrative requires the artist as a narrator-protagonist.' Having built up the artist's voice, as a means of reaching new and active audiences, the institution will not benefit from its silence.

left Mischa Kuball, *Private Light/Public Light*, 1998

In this project Kuball gradually replaced public lights on the streets of São Paulo with domestic fixtures. In the *Private Light* phase of the project, Kuball moved to the interior site. Standardized lamps replaced private fixtures, which had been removed from different homes and exhibited; in a certain way they thus represented their owners. The private settings, before and after swapping light sources, were documented in photographs. As private tastes gave way to standardized lighting, one language to another, individuality and identity were brought into conflict with civil society.

left Kendell Geers, *Poetic Justice*, 1999

The South African artist's work was concerned with the political heritage of the apartheid regime in South Africa. His work uses television sets and packing materials, pallets, cables, plugs, etc. The themes of the short video loops were intentionally disturbing. Geers wished to evoke the uncanny and a feeling of danger.

Beat Streuli
above *Portraits*, 2002
below *Billboard Sydney*, 1998
Streuli's work is concerned with erasing history and difference, changing images into a flat universalism. The work deliberately uses the language and techniques of advertising. Duraclear images are usually placed in main urban shopping areas or on building concourses. The works consist of larger-than-life portraits of anonymous passers-by who are depicted in a state of deep introspection and juxtaposed with their actual surroundings.

right Tobias Rehberger, *Brancusi*, 1997
Rehberger combines art, architecture and design, focusing
on creations for immediate consumption – instantaneous
works that paraphrase the dogma of modernistic actuality
and question issues of commercialization. The artist designed
an advertisement for a Berlin gallery, which appeared in art
magazines. He then presented the advertisement to a textile
designer, who used it as a pattern for garments worn by
gallery staff during an art fair. Subsequently, the gallery
used the same advertisement as a model for the exhibition
'Brancusi' in 1997. The two-dimensional layout was translated
onto three-dimensional surfaces, which could be interpreted
as 1970s-style furniture or as autonomous sculptures. In this
work Rehberger renounced his authorship, concentrating
like a manager on co-ordinating different processes, thus
reducing hierarchies, but also focusing on the variability
of interpretation and content.

right Françoise Bassand, *3D*, 1998
A number of artists (105 in total) were invited to modify
the interior and exterior of a former private clinic in Zurich,
Switzerland. These works were then 'morphed' by other
artists. One of the participators was the Swiss artist Françoise
Bassand, who created a room inspired by the 1970s wall
decoration in the staircase of the building. Bassand then
invited five more artists, who had been working on the
project, to interact with the existing installation.

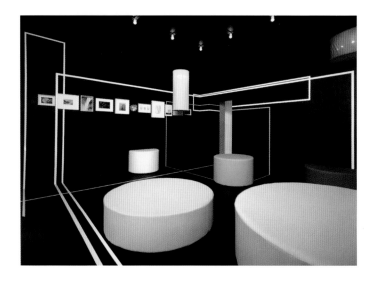

Fabrice Gygi
right *Sans nul titre*, 1998
below *Tribunal*, 1999
The Swiss artist Fabrice Gygi fabricates portable structures
such as platforms, constructions of metal and plywood,
tarpaulins, tents made from foam rubber padding and inflated,
oversized airbags from industrially produced materials. The
notion of displacement is aimed at the institution destined to
host the pieces. Gygi has acquired a keen awareness of the
workings of authoritarian power, the ways in which freedom
and control, security and threat interact. His installations
communicate a deep-seated mistrust of any form of finality
where the meaning of the work emerges from an exchange
with the physical and mental context in which they are made.

left Luchezar Boyadjiev, *Gazebo*, 1996
Boyadjiev placed four cinema chairs
on a stone platform of local stone from
a cleared site, hired from the farmer
who owned the land. Vegetation
between two private fields was cut
down to create an opening revealing a
view towards the city. This construction
evoked a metaphor of the cinematic
frame and revealed the artificiality of
perception, thus allowing for the
contemplation of landscape to appear
as a culturally constructed utopia.

opposite below Bob & Roberta Smith, Jessica Voorsanger, *Joe Amrhein at the LCCA*, 2001
Bob & Roberta Smith inaugurated the Leytonstone Center for Contemporary Art in his back garden with the artist and curator Jessica Voorsanger. The garden shed acts like a parody of the modernist art gallery, the so-called 'white cube'.
A series of conferences, actions and exhibitions have been held in the equivalent of a garden shed from which they deliberately comment on the institution and undermine its authority .

below Michael Smith and Joshua White, *The QuinQuag*, Arts and Wellness Centre (touring exhibition), 2002
Combining the irreconcilable language of corporate entrepreneurship and New Age spiritualism, the New York based artists Michael Smith and Joshua White created an elaborate installation about a fictional art colony. The installation took the form of a travelling exhibition, displaying apparently authentic photographs, craft objects , self-help videos and artworks. Through the use of elements familiar from news stories and historical narratives, the viewer was immersed in a fictional world.

below Jorge Pardo, *Pier*, 1997
In many of his works the Cuban artist Jorge Pardo makes explicit reference to the exhibition site, combining the exhibition venue, the artwork and the conditions of its reception. In Münster, Germany, in 1997, Pardo constructed a 131-foot-long (40 m) pier, which led to an open pavilion and a viewing platform with steps to a lake. Pardo often highlights the utilitarian aspect of his installations, making furniture and arrangements in order to focus on a distinction between art and design.

above Mark Dion, *Alexander Wilson Studio*, 1999
The American artist Mark Dion has been involved with the history of collection, classification and display as practised by scientific institutions such as natural history museums or pre-museum archives (*Wunderkammern* and Cabinets of Curiosity), often collaborating with museums like the Tate, London. Using the strategy of imitation, the artist assumes the role of a scientific researcher and explorer in order to analyze the ideological foundations and the myths of objectivity and neutrality of such institutions. His environments include 'realistic facts' which are theatrically exaggerated and fictionalized.

opposite Ayşe Erkmen, *Sculptures on Air*, 1997
Antique sculptures from a museum collection were carried by helicopter from the museum's storage place, located some distance from the main building, to the roof of the museum. Each time, the helicopter carried a new sculpture and took away the previous one. A sculpture stayed on the roof until the next one arrived. This action of the Turkish artist Ayşe Erkmen was repeated once or twice a week at Münster Sculpture Projects, 1997.

below Hans Haacke, *Der Bevölkerung (To the Population)*, 1999–2000

The work consisted of an installation in the northern open-air courtyard of the Berlin Reichstag (German Parliament building) and a web site. At the invitation of the Bundestag the artist invited the 669 members of the German parliament to fill an oblong wooden trough with 100 kilogrammes of earth from their respective electoral districts. The dedication *Der Bevölkerung* was chosen to contrast with the words on the portal of the Reichstag, *Dem deutschen Volke* (To the German People). The dedication was designed with the same typographic font and size. Haacke interpreted the writing *Dem deutschen Volke* as 'nationalistic' because it failed to take into account people from other countries. The project sparked debate between the political parties in the German parliament, with 260 voting for the project, 258 against it and 31 abstaining. All the Conservative parties rejected the project.

above and opposite Christo and Jeanne-Claude, *Wrapped Reichstag*, Berlin, 1971–95

In 1945, after the battle for Berlin, the Reichstag was in ruins. It was restored however between 1957 and 1971. After the fall of the Berlin wall in 1989, the Reichstag regained its status as the seat of the German parliament. Already in 1961 Christo had created a collage with photographs and a text, entitled *Project for a Wrapped Public Building*. The idea of the *Wrapped Reichstag* was developed between 1971 and 1995, during which time the Christos spent many months lobbying in Bonn, talking personally to 352 MPs, to convince the German parliament to grant permission for the wrapping of the building. Permission was refused three times, in 1977, 1981 and 1987. Finally, the

Bundestag voted to grant permission on 25 February 1994. On 18 June 1995 at 5 a.m. the unfurling of the fabric began simultaneously on the four façades. Custom-made cushions placed between the cages supported the rolls of fabric, keeping them in a horizontal position and facilitating the unrolling. For safety reasons, every panel was temporarily roped tight in case of a sudden wind. The entire roof and both inner courtyards were wrapped with 100,000 square metres of 70 recyclable, aluminum-coated, fabric panels. The rooftop wrapping was secured by blue ropes which in turn were attached to 270 anchors on the roof and weighted on the sidewalks around the building. The Reichstag remained wrapped for fourteen days.

Christo and Jeanne-Claude have completed many projects, including wrapping buildings, surrounding islands with floating fabric skirts and fencing in miles of coastline and inland hills. All these have taken years of planning. The sale of early works of the 1950s and 1960s, as well as the preparatory drawings, fund their projects. In fact, drawings and collages add to the development of ideas and serve as pre-documents which can be compared with actuality. The whole process is part of the work, be it meetings with town planners, site owners, court hearings, bureaucratic redtape and the installation of the work. All Christo and Jeanne-Claude's projects are site-specific and time-based (often only being up for a few days or weeks) and can be looked upon as large-scale site installations.

below Anish Kapoor, *Tarantara*, 1999
Anish Kapoor's installation at the
BALTIC, Newcastle, in 1999 was part of
of a programme of commissioned works

entitled 'B4B' in collaboration with the
region's cultural organizations. The new
Art Centre was still under construction
and would only be completed in 2002.

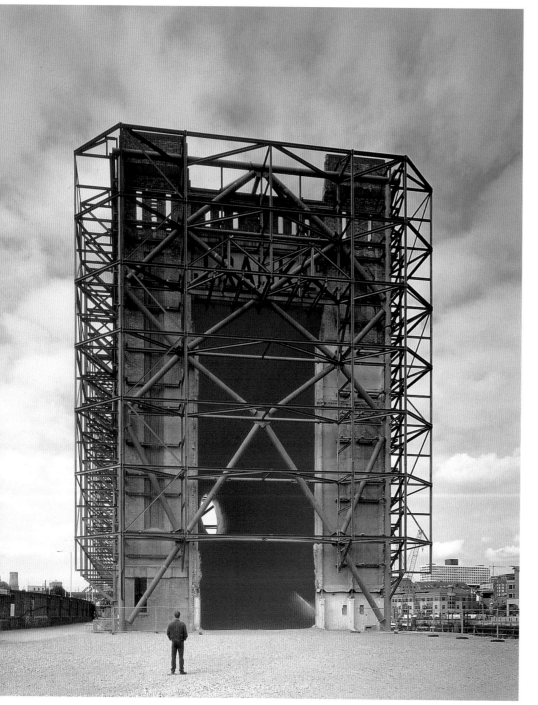

opposite above Thomas Hirschhorn,
World Airport/ Flugplatz Welt, 1999
The Swiss artist Thomas Hirschhorn's
works are epic and detailed displays.
He chooses disposable materials,
cardboard, tape and tin foil, which he
uses as umbilical cords to connect the
environments. The deliberate use of
crude materials coupled with the
monumental subject matter produces
a metaphorically fragile world which
questions the hypocrisy of political
power structures and the museum
as an institution. Hirschhorn deliberately
employs what he himself describes as
cheap tricks and stupid things in order
to humorously undermine power.

opposite below Micah Lexier,
*Ampersand: A Project for the
Sheppard/Leslie Subway Station*, 2002
Every wall of the new Sheppard/Leslie
Subway Station was covered with one
of 17,000 custom-printed tiles. The
tiles bore the handwriting of different
members of the public, spelling the
words 'Sheppard' and 'Leslie'. During
May 1997 the public were invited to fill
out ballots which were then enlarged
and turned into individual tiles. A total
of 3,500 different samples where
selected and made into an edition of five
tiles. The work played off the dichotomy
between community and individuality
and was a homage to the unique yet
anonymous contribution of those
who participated.

right Daniel Pflumm, *Ohne Titel* (Untitled), 1998
In the early 1990s the Swiss artist Daniel Pflumm set up
a series of lifestyle spaces, like clubs, creating fashionable
forums for art as action. He renegotiated the idea of corporate
identity, appropriating visual indicators, symbols from the
world of the media, logos, spear points of image production
in a live situation. Using the elevations of various venues
around the world Pflumm installed illuminated signs of his
logo. This underlines the artist's mission to include a corporate
symbol which lives on after the exhibition is over and leaves
a permanent brand on each institution.

below Barbara Bloom, *Pictures from the Floating World*, 1995
Hundreds of male and female oriental masks of stone-coloured
plaster were arranged in pairs on a red floor painted the colour
of Chinese lacquer. A vitrine was placed in the middle of a
carved wooden bridge spanning the whole space. Six
magnifying lenses were mounted into the glass top of the
vitrine and positioned over six grains of rice which each bore a

miniature erotic Japanese image. The installation focused on
the theme of scale, composed as it was of elements both
extremely large and small. The beauty of the forbidden,
censored erotic Japanese Shunga prints contrasted with the
large field of masks on the floor.

right and below Tatsurou Bashi (alias Tazro Niscino), *Villa Victoria*, 2002 Bashi's *Villa Victoria* was a hotel room, built around an existing monument of Queen Victoria, which could be hired for the night. It was commissioned by the International 2002 exhibition for the Liverpool Biennial. The exterior resembled a building site, but it concealed a highly finished and comfortable interior. The scale of the monumental sculpture in a domestic setting drew attention to the difference between public and private space.

left Micah Lexier, *The Hall of Names*, 1996

The work by the Canadian artist Micah Lexier consisted of one thousand laser-cut stainless steel names which were hung in a series of chains in the 800-foot-long (244 m) Grand Concourse of the National Trade Centre in Toronto. From a submission of 6,435 names from over 65 communities across Canada, the Canadian artist randomly drew 1000 names to be included in the work. Lexier's work is preoccupied with the audience's participation through anonymous processes.

above Stefan Brüggemann, *Capitalism and Schizophrenia*, 2003

The Mexican artist Stefan Brüggemann's work makes an ironic reference to the writings of the French philosophers Deleuze and Guattari. The vast styrofoam letters were produced and shown at the same factory in Puerto Rico, thus combining the activities of making and exhibiting in one site. Brüggemann's work employs techniques of quotation to comment on the history of ideas.

right Elmgreen & Dragset, *Powerless Structures*, *Fig. 111*, 2001; below *Taking Place*, 2001–2002

In their work the Scandinavian duo Michael Elmgreen and Ingar Dragset created a series of white cubes, which were displaced, fragmented and manipulated. The artists had staged unexpected clashes between the aesthetic of the white cube and that of sites of gay sexuality. The work showed not only the powerlessness and flexibility of all structures – white walls do not have to carry the kind of transcendental significance they are sometimes assigned – but also a gay 'infiltration' of modernist aesthetic.

Miguel Leal
right *Bunker Project (1996–99), Museum of Modern Strategy — International Department Room*, 1999
below *Bunker Project (1996–99), Museum of Modern Strategy – Frozen objects: Producing Contents; Showcases and Institutional Objects*, 1999

The *Bunker Project* of the Portuguese artist Miguel Leal is an ongoing work which has been shown in different locations around the world, varying its configurations at each site. The *Museum of Modern Strategy* (*MOMS*) was set up by the artist as a critique of the museum and its power base. It was planned on the basis of a fictional and heterodox structure, seeking to use its ambiguous status to largely justify its existence. *MOMS* is part of a vaster project with the generic name of *Bunker*. The first classification of *Bunker* included the *Analytical Department*, the *Art Department*, the *International Department*, the *Digital Department* and also the *Revolting Museum Project*; the second category included the projećts *Bird's Eye*, *Night Watch* and *Warin Theory*.

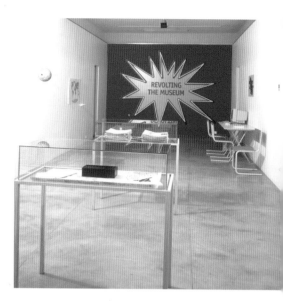

above and below Joëlle Tuerlinckx,
In Real Time, Space Parts/ Night Cabin/Solar-room, 2002
An announcement is heard as the spectator enters this space. A female voice draws attention to the 100 per cent natural daylight conditions in the gallery and assures the audience that any changes are due to bad weather and climatic conditions. The Belgian artist Joëlle Tuerlinckx comments on gallery decorum and manners, where art ends and the everyday begins. Everything in her work is in transit, between display and stockpile, gallery installation and skip. Tuerlinckx's work is not a commentary on art, but more on small perceptual shifts that change our understanding of reality.

Dutton/Peacock, *Apocotropes*, 1996–97
The British artists Steve Dutton and
Percy Peacock began collaborating on
projects in 1996. Much of their work
had involved the use of large-scale,
often inverted or revolving photographs.
Three 6-foot-square (0.5 m square)
photographs on MDF proposed the
artist's studio as an artwork in various
stages of production. The photographs
effectively documented the processes
of their own production, within which
the location of the 'work' is difficult to
define. The status of photographs as
props, complex artworks, or factual
documents is here problematized.

left above and below Michel François,
Bureau Augmenté (Enlarged Office), 1998
The work of the Belgian artist Michel
François transformed the gallery into a
chaotic office: computers, empty bullet
casings and capsules, a heap of metal
coins spilled onto the floor, stacks of
newspapers littering the carpet,
primary coloured numbers and letters
seeming to float on the walls, loose
wires dangling from the ceiling. The
busy effect of clutter and excess was
accentuated by the incessant flashing
of a white fluorescent light and several
videos perpetually playing in various
corners of the gallery. The sound of
frogs emanated from hidden speakers,
objects came apart, spilled over,
scattered and separated in a series
of gestures that explored chaos, order,
dispersion and restoration. The
installation mirrored the disintegration
of the gallery as an inert white cube,
revealing the tension and deadening
repetition of our daily working lives and
finally reflecting a Kafkaesque view of
corporate life.

below Dutton/Peacock, *Europe*, 1999
In this work Dutton and Peacock threw the contents of a vacuum cleaner into the air at their studio and a series of photographs documented the event. These sequences were concerned with the use of the studio as a space of ambiguous production. One photograph was chosen to be inverted and made into a postcard. The resulting card was then widely distributed around Europe.

below and right below John Newling, *Weight*, 1998
This work by the British artist John Newling examines the relationship between literal and metaphorical value by revealing human traces extracted from coins. Ten laboratory assistants weighed and cleaned fifty thousand two-pence coins at the gallery, which had been transformed into a well-equipped laboratory. As part of this pseudo-scientific method, tents erected on an adjacent roof acted as evaporation sites for the cleaning chemicals. All the residue of human touch was removed from the coins and stored in jars placed on ten laboratory tables in the gallery and could be viewed at the end of the experiment. Calculations demonstrated that the dirt on the coins had a measurable value, equated to the weight of seven pence, a magic number. Newling's work offered an intriguing exploration of the relationships between people and objects of financial and cultural worth and consequently questioned value systems.

below right Henrik Plenge Jakobsen, *Diary of Plasma*, 1995–96 Experimental science as an ecstasy of limits is the subject of this ongoing video/publication/installation project. The installation uses fake scientific elements and real laboratory materials, such as a urine reactor. The core of the piece is the text, of which the plot mirrors Mary Shelley's Frankenstein story, a young scientist who works with an undefined biotech product and has been deadlocked in a blind alley of psychosis. The work counters the utopian expectations of experimental science. Jakobsen's art constitutes a tenacious intervention in the structures that determine systems. It throws doubt on the human body as matter and on its relation to authority and the social context.

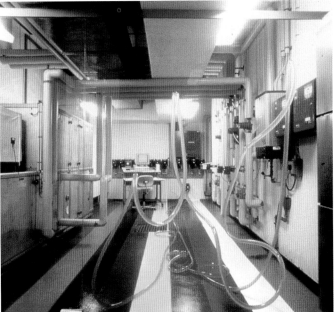

right Martin Creed, *Work No 270 'The Lights Off'*, 2001
The spectator's gaze is directed through the darkness of
the empty space to a sales certificate on the gallery wall.
'The Lights Off' perfectly expresses the conceptual position of
the British artist and Turner Prize Winner, which is marked
by sublime humour and an often paradoxical pragmatism.

below Renato Niemis, *[;]*, 1994
The British artist Renato Niemis built a wooden catwalk, an
isolated, floating path, on which visitors were allowed to walk
and stand. The piece frames the setting of the exhibition space
by focusing the viewer's attention on the relationship between
the viewer and the viewed.

left and below Hew Locke, *Cardboard Palace*, 2002
This was a vast architectural construction which investigated
the traditions of British culture and heritage, resonating
with issues surrounding the nation's monarchy. Locke created
an apparently chaotic structure, in which visitors negotiated
loosely defined areas. As viewers passed through this
fantastical maze, they witnessed a series of cardboard
images of the British royal family, delicately intertwined
with cut-out texts alluding to packaging, export and
commodity culture.

exchange and interaction

In the seventies and eighties, we lived in a society of spectacle, in the nineties in the society of participants, and we are now developing a 'society of interactors'.

It is necessary to explore the assertion that the spectator, the viewer of an artwork, is now an interactor and the ways in which this affects the artist and their chosen forms of address. What strategies do they employ to facilitate the desired interaction and exchange, and in what way does new Installation work address such issues?

The opening of the Palais de Tokyo in Paris in 2002 was welcomed as a new 'site of contemporary creation'. Nicolas Bourriaud, joint project director, put forward his idea about 'relational aesthetics', which sees art's response to an ever more regimented society to introduce 'interactivity, conviviality and relationality'. He proposed an art in which objects are catalysts generating communicative processes.

Rirkrit Tiravanija, from Argentina, is one such artist. According to Paolo Bianchi, co-curator of the exhibition *LKW* (from *Lebenskunstwerke*, 'life artworks'), held in Bregenz, 2000, Tiravanija 'mistrusts objects, putting his faith into that which takes place between people, in communication.' Tiravanija's collaborative installation *Bon Voyage, Monsieur Tiravanija. Opel Blitz* with German artist

Franz Ackermann consisted in a remodelled truck containing a library of guidebooks, together with a series of monitors showing videos by the two artists on their travels. 'The truck provides new, more open, more flexible and more spontaneous structures,' stated the artists. Elsewhere in the exhibition, the Danish Collective N55 constructed sleeping arrangements, a kitchen and a waste-disposal system. The work focused on the economics and activities of everyday lives and needs.

A different approach to alternative lifestyle culture is taken by the Dutch group Atelier van Lieshout, who rely on a factory-like environment to generate their projects. Their catalogue raisonné, *A Manual* (1997), shows their full range of artistic products, along with detailed instructions on their manufacture for the audience. The large, glass fibre, reinforced polyester environments are often portable. The vehicle subject appears frequently and provides an art that makes a virtue of its mobile nature.

Tiravanija and Ackermann's collaboration focuses on the 'nomadic' element of place, as the site of the work changes continuously and each location visited by the truck relies on a different audience, offering alternative readings of the installation. Van Lieshout's modules also eschew the notion of a fixed site through their utopian living spaces which prioritize human activity. The location becomes simply the place where interaction occurs. Indeed, these modules invariably look practical for everyday use, yet at the same time appear as if they do not quite belong anywhere. In this way, their restlessness is underlined by the suspicion that they are 'non-places', totally mobile yet essentially rootless.

The questions of mobility and exchange with different audiences have come to dominate the practice of Installation. The two terms are linked, since the mobile or flexible site enables artists to reach a greater diversity of viewers. The works of Spanish artist Alicia Framis and Mexican-born Jose Dávila provide examples of these developments by involving their audiences in activities and exchanges, which in turn raise questions about the institutionalized behaviour patterns of viewers towards art. Framis's *Blood Sushi Bar* (2000) invited visitors to partake of food in a highly designed environment, while Dávila's *Open Studio* (2000) included discussion on the nature of artistic production in the open air. The installation was a set resembling an artist's private working space. The studio, or indeed its absence, had become the exhibit, as it generated nothing beyond itself, other than a critique or discussion of the traditional studio which has provided a crucial focus for artists over centuries.

Many contemporary Installation artists today have abandoned the studio, preferring to work on a 'project' basis whenever required. If artists are invited to make installations for a gallery, the given space takes on the temporary guise of a studio. This shift from the traditional space where art is produced is compounded by the spread of electronic communication and international mobility. The result is the production of an increasingly restless kind of artwork. 'Thus, if the artist is successful,' writes Miwon Kwon, 'he or she travels constantly as a freelancer, often working on more than one site-specific project at a time, globetrotting as a guest, tourist, adventurer, temporary in-house critic, or pseudo ethnographer.'

As Installation has moved into the centre of artistic practice and with it, embraced its constant mobility, it has reached new types of audiences, resulting in different modes of audience participation. Installation provides places for exchange in which the audience becomes an integral part of the work, as shown in these examples. The artist, as a rule does not perform to the audience, rather it is this open-ended interaction with the potential of the real-life situation that mark the viewer's experience.

This theme of exchange may also take the form of commercial activity. The British artist Mark Povell's exhibition *Supply & Demand* (2001) at the Museum of Installation, London, invited visitors to make drawings on computer terminals, which were then turned into three-dimensional cardboard objects. The transition from drawing to object was cemented by the filling out of a contract between the artist and the interactor and on receipt of the object the interactor was asked to pay an appropriate sum to the artist. Here art became a non-essential 'service provision' to the spectator. According to Kwon, 'The artist as an overspecialised aesthetic object maker has been anachronistic for a long time already. What they provide now, rather than produce, are aesthetic, often "critical-artistic" services.' This absence of art objects can be seen in the work of the British artist Simon Moretti. *A Space For Conversation* (2000) consisted of circular carpets laid on the access-ramp of the Tate Modern museum in London. The installation created an intimacy in a busy thoroughfare, as visitors were invited to sit on the carpets and participate in a drawing project devised by the artist. While Moretti asked viewers to participate in producing, the level of public interaction required in Surasi Kusolwong's *Happy Berlin (Free Massage)* of 2001, was simply to submit to the free service provided by the artist's professional crew: a massage. Kusolwong, from Thailand, promotes an egalitarian and inclusive art, while looking after his visitors' needs. The participation in a form of 'game' in Moretti's Installation led participants to indulge in seemingly open play which stimulated inventiveness. The media theorist Marshall McLuhan had predicted the growing desire within post-industrial culture for playing games, an argument which he extends into the world of scientific research: 'The world of science has become quite self-conscious about the play element in its endless experiments with models of situations otherwise unobservable.'

It is through the shared mode of 'play' that artists and scientists have found perhaps the most intriguing partnerships. The depth of research provided in this field has attracted a number of artists to form new relationships and collaborations. In particular, the absolute necessity of process and play in scientific research provides a useful parallel for artistic practice. The Belgian-born artist Carsten Höller initially trained as a scientist. His installations combine the rigorous language of science with playful experimentation. Wim Delvoye, also from Belgium, shares Höller's engagement with research, culminating in what is arguably his most provocative work *Cloaca* (2001) shown at the New Museum of Contemporary Art in New York and in Switzerland. The work was a complex machine which commented both on the methods of manufacture, as well as on our revulsion towards bodily effluvia. The machine replicated the human digestive tract and was fed a careful diet of food prepared in the adjacent kitchen. This passed through several chemical stages of 'digestion', each part clearly visible to the audience, until the apparatus produced perfect examples of stools. The work also played with the idea of participation, in that it needed to be continually fed to produce editions which the audience could take away. The audience was offered the very thing it does not want as a by-product of the artistic process. While *Cloaca* uses scientific methods and manufacturing technology to his own ends, *Polar* (2000), a collaboration between Marko Peljhan and Olaf Nicolai, sought to utilize science as a means of disclosing new relationships between art and technology. Exhibited in Tokyo, it was represented by an installation that revealed the internet in real time. The artists compared it to the sentient sea in the Stanislav Lem story which became the basis for *Solaris* by Andrej Tarkovsky. Peljhan, from Slovenia, and Nicolai, from Germany stated: 'We wanted to create an interface between the matrix and the human senses and body.'

To those who would believe that social interactivity might provide an unproblematic solution for the future of art, Bourriaud offers a word of caution: 'Now that the ideology of the internet links and continuous contact has come to pervade the globalised economy...how much critical radicality is left to work based on sociality and conviviality?' He champions instead a type of exhibition that addresses 'a new problematic, that of the coexistence of humans, objects and forms, which generates a specific meaning.' The exhibition is not simply a means for conviviality, but to Bourriaud it acts as 'a cognitive tool', a way of generating meaning and content.

The German artist Christian Jankowski's installations appears to bear out Bourriaud's argument. The encounter with others leads to a series of dialogues which transform the outcome of his works. In *Mein erstes Buch: Inszeniertes Schreiben* (My First Book: Staged Writing, 1998) Jankowski sits in a gallery and invites a range of specialist consultants to aid him in writing his first novel. The artist is not 'performing', instead he is absorbed in the process of writing or in discussions.

The question of process as a form of dialogue between artists, collaborators and audiences is of paramount importance to many contemporary installations. What is intended here is to suggest that the form of the artwork has become secondary to its journey and duration. Fluidity has become a buzzword in the new millennium and is indicative of a lack of boundaries. It is unsurprising that artists are keen to work with flexible boundaries, a desire that begins to explain the rise of the art-project which can take any form, occur anywhere and, as Rirkrit Tiravanija states, include 'lots of people'. Moreover, the development of the audience as a site, that is, the centre and meaning of the work, has resulted in a shift from aesthetic and art-historical issues to a concern with the social integration of the installation. The cross-fertilization between disciplines, the exchange between curators and artists and the interaction with audiences as a means of generating the work itself have all been instrumental in shaping Installation art. The Chinese curator Hou Hanru states that 'we are contributing, directly and jointly, to the development of situations'. Such 'situations' based on exchange and interaction bear witness to the open-ended and inclusive approach to Installation art in the new millennium.

above and right Cai Guo-Qiang, *Cultural Melting Bath*, 1997
The Chinese artist transported 30 tons of rock from Diangsu in China to New York. Using traditional *feng shui* on the site, the massive Taihusu rocks were each carefully selected for their characteristics of stimulating the flow of energy in the space, and bestowing beneficial *qi* on the museum and its visitors. The clusters of rocks also contained a Chinese medicinal herbal bath. Cai sees his therapeutic *Cultural Melting Bath* as a metaphor for social healing. In his work he used the term 'melting pot', inviting individuals from disparate backgrounds to bathe together, fusing East and West.

opposite page Carsten Nicolai and Marko Peljhan, *Polar*, 2000
This collaborative piece by the Slovenian artist Pelijhan and the German artist Nicolai was produced by Canon Art Lab in Tokyo; they were awarded a golden Nica at Ars Electronica for their work. *Polar* works as a tool to experience the network in real time. It is a machine that translates and makes visible not only the information flow, but also the meaning of data that is found in the networks. Peljhan described the work as follows: 'We envisioned the space as totally connected, as a complex tactile – matrix.' This enables the audience to experience the data in the global and local networks in a completely immersing yet cognitive way. The work was inspired by the notion of the sentient ocean in Stanislaw Lem's novel and the film *Solaris* by the director Andrej Tarkovsky. 'We wanted to create an interface between the matrix and the human senses and body.'

above and below N55, *Hygiene System Extended*, 1999
This collective WC, an object referring to a kind of minimalism with social consciousness, was created by N55, a Danish artist collective, founded as a group in 1994. The experiments focused on an examination of social conventions and issues of power, which influence the audience's perception. This social experiment in the everyday included confronting people in a combination of leisure and work environments.

above ECM 323, *Test Sites*, 1999
The group of artists ECM 323 created a set up which surveyed and analyzed experimental sound, virtual imagery and individual perceptions. The primary theme of the project was how sound can influence form and vice versa. The piece focused on the investigation of an audience's response to Binaural brain frequencies, the manifestation of wave forms as visual information, and the production and evolution of acoustic signals realized as electronic feedback.

opposite above Rirkrit Tiravanija, *Untitled, (He Promised)*, 2002
This Argentinian-born artist was brought up in Thailand, Canada and Argentina. His work fuses art and life, from music to cooking. The performative and interactive projects pursue cultural boundaries and themes such as nomadism, global art and the internet. He has been working on a democratic art magazine in which contributors can publish their own work around the world, without editorial restrictions.

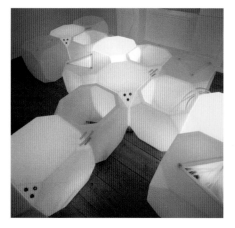

opposite below Carlos Amorales, *Producion/Calidad*, 2002
The Mexican artist Amorales created a metaphoric *maquiladora*, a cost-saving business venture which seeks to attract corporations, usually American, to bring manual jobs to Mexican border towns. Amorales's work suggested a warehouse by a geometric grid marked on the museum floor, using famous artworks from the permanent collection, some in boxes for shipping, others on view for the public. The work raised socio-political questions about production and consumption and explored the issue of the museum as a storage area but also as a participant in the globalization of the art trade.

above Keith Tyson, *Supercollider*, 2002
The exhibition title by the British artist
Keith Tyson, was derived from the slang
name for the CERN particle accelerator
in Geneva. A giant glowing sphere, two
metres in diameter, gradually changed
colour as it reacted to heating and
cooling elements inside. *Field of
Heaven Long Shot Magnet* presented
a motorized model which made real
pieces of planets and meteorites,
including a chunk of the moon. These
rotated around each other in an orbital
arrangement that would never occur
in reality. Tyson's ongoing fascination
with scientific ideas and philosophical
arguments leads to a desire to
experiment with information, drawing
objects and devising systems that
question our existence.

Carsten Höller
above and right *Glück*, 1996
opposite above *Skop*, 1996
opposite far right *Riesenpsychotank*,
1999
The Belgian-born artist's work is based
on his training as a biologist and
explores theories of evolution which

regard human sentiments, such as
love, primarily as strategies for the
reproduction of genetic material.
Formally, his installations remind
us of laboratory structures in which
it is possible to fly around in a circle,
immerse one's head in an aquarium or
to speed down a slope in a soundproofed

sledge. *Glück* features an experimental obstacle course in which visitors see themselves as subjects and conductors of experiments at the same time. For the 'Sanatorium' exhibition, he created *Riesenpsychotank*, a large, semi-transparent container, offering the audience the chance to bathe in public.

above Alicia Framis, *Blood Sushi Bank*, 2000
'Art can occur anywhere; it is not the space that makes the
event but the event that creates the space,' states the Spanish
artist Alicia Framis. *Blood Sushi Bank* was an interactive and
highly stylized bar which offered food for thought to the
audience. The service provided by the artist gave visitors
an experience in which they could participate, thus questioning
their perception of artistic production.

left and below Mark Povell, *Supply and Demand*, 2001
British artist Mark Povell devised a computer programme which generated templates for a system of simple three-dimensional objects; these templates were designed to be customized by the visitor to produce new objects. The *Supply and Demand* team undertook to manufacture versions of these objects over the course of the exhibition period as part of a 'contract' with the visitor. The visitor was asked to offer an 'interpretation' in exchange for the object and equivalent to their estimation of its value.

below left Surasi Kusolwong, *Happy Berlin (Free Massage)*, 2001
In the 2nd Berlin Biennale, Kusolwong used Thai silk curtains
to divide the museum space and opened it as a massage salon.
Almost every day during the two-month show, museum goers
were invited to have a free traditional Thai Massage. While
waiting, they could relax on comfortable mattresses watching
the film *The Mask of Zorro*.

below right Surasi Kusolwong, *Emotional Machine (VW)*, 2001
The Thai artist Surasi Kusolwong focuses on creating spaces
for exchange. He is well known for his large-scale market
installations where Thai products are sold at low prices.
He describes his work as 'Poor Minimal' and juxtaposes
free massages, lottery games, dismantled parts of cars,
classic design furniture and vending machines offering drinks.
Visitors to his exhibitions enjoy relaxing, humorous scenarios.
In this work, commissioned for the 2002 Gwangju Biennale,
'Pause', Kusolwong displayed a stripped-down Volkswagen
Beetle which was hung upside down from the ceiling, turning
it into a swing. Inside the car a wooden floor was built up with
soft mattresses and pillows providing the visitors with a bed
to lie on. The visitors were able to watch the film *Harry Potter*
in comfort. The floor was covered with a green carpet and
potted plants, creating an artificial city garden, vending
machines provided free soft drinks and chocolate and a bank
of computers gave free internet access.

above and opposite Navin Rawanchaikul, *I [love] TAXI*, 2001
The Thai artist Navin Rawanchaikul used the universal space
of the taxi as the physical container for his mobile gallery.
The audience of the work was literally transported to the
destination of their choice. This dialogue between the taxi as
the art receptacle and the driver as the willing artist-host finds
its partner in the fare-paying participant. Rawanchaikul adopts
a new strategy for art production by taking a common activity
and appropriating it as an art strategy.

right Alexander Pilis, *Architecture Parallax: Blind Date*, 1998
The image expresses the discourse underlying *Architecture Parallax: Collective Intelligence*. According to the Brazilan artist Pilis, embedded within a frozen moment of love and dependency are positions in motion, with no discernible fixed point of reference. From here, an architectural conversation emerges to articulate differences and impossibilities where the depth of field has collapsed.

top right Maywa Denki, *Hall in Love*, 1999
Maywa Denki combines exhibitions, live stage performances, music, videos, writing, merchandising toys, stationary and electrical devices. This work was a live sound performance using their products. Each one was stylishly designed and modified as a toy to be mass-produced in the marketplace. They became so popular among young people that some of Japan's major toy stores set up Maywa Denki departments.

above Henrik Håkansson, *Tomorrow and Tonight*, 1999–2000
The Swedish artist Henrik Håkansson uses video and closed-circuit surveillance systems to record the behaviour of wild life. He incorporates the incompatible combination of club music, youth culture and ritualized entertainment with the natural sciences, and ends up with a visual mix which is at once utopian and dystopic. The environments of this modern-day Doctor Doolittle establish the possible mixing of the characteristics of one subculture with another. In this work the artist proposed the proliferation of roof gardens as 'landing-strips' for insects and other wildlife.

below Carsten Nicolai, *Model zur Visualisierung von Sound* (Model for Visualizing Sound), 1999
The German artist Carsten Nicolai has developed a keen interest in the psychological and physical effects of sound. The artist's work for the Liverpool Biennial in 1999 was an extension of his research on the possible bodily effects of vibration. Sampled tones, modem beeps, and telephone clicks were organized into loops to produce minimalist cycles of abstract sound. This resulted in a manifestation of the invisible energy of electricity: the acoustic trace of an intangible commodity.

left Chris Grottick, *New Clear Days*, 1998
In 'Turbulence' (1998) by the British artist Chris Grottick, a sequence of scans made from air pressure charts taken by a satellite over Northern Europe every six hours over a period of a year were erratically reanimated using an apparatus measuring gusts of wind from the street outside the exhibition space.

below Paola Pivi, *E*, 2001
The Italian artist Paola Pivi's interactive installation simultaneously triggered both attraction and repulsion. The construction was a cylindrical metal structure, made of innumerable vertical nylon wires to which nails were attached, the points turned towards the visitor. When these were approached, sensors became activated which made all the tips shift in one collective, threatening movement. The fragility of the structure and the delicacy of the movement itself, however, seemed to restrict the action and thus negated the potential aggression of the piece.

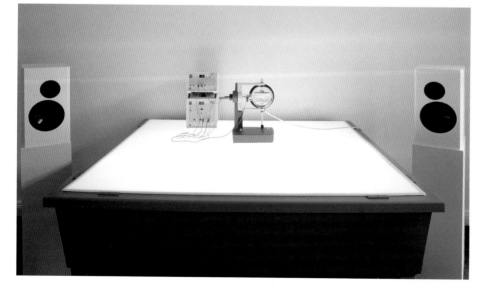

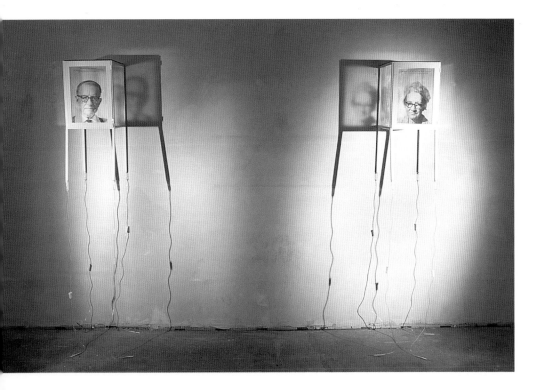

left Adriano Guimarães and Fernando Guimarães, *The Theatre of Installation*, 2000
This work by the Brazilian theatre directors Adriano and Fernando Guimarães dealt with presentation strategies of the stage and the gallery. Their interactive elements of their staging add an immersive dimension to their work.

left Angela Bulloch *'Macro-World': One Hour3 and Canned*, 2002
The complex pixel works of the Canadian artist Angela Bulloch, such as *'Macro-World'*, uses digitally controlled light boxes to probe the interactive relations between the production and reception of visual images. The artist uses the pixel patterns of selected scenes out of films and television programmes. The basic idea behind these works is that the pixel, normally the smallest component of digital image information, is massively enlarged. Through the exaggerating shift of scale, the grid system of the pixel boxes controls the viewer's visual and kinaesthetic experience, submerging the viewer and the space in a dynamic, coloured luminous space.

Christoph Büchel, *Untitled*, 2001
For the inaugural exhibition at
Maccarone Inc., 2001, in New York City,
the Swiss artist Christoph Büchel made
an installation that took over the entire
2152 square feet (200 m²) of the gallery
space. The artist created a labyrinth
of rooms ranging from a waiting room,
kitchen, bomb shelter, schoolroom and
jail cell which visitors had to crawl
through to experience.

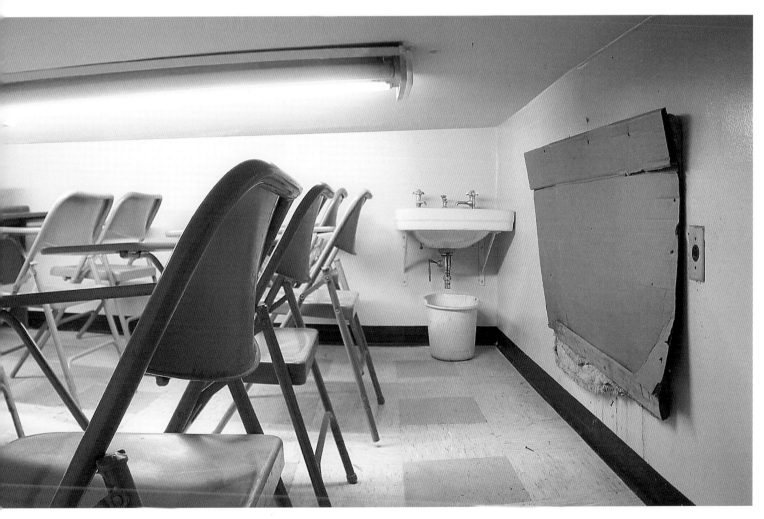

Atelier van Lieshout **above** *Compostopia*, 2002
opposite below right *Maxi Capsule Luxus*, 2002
The Dutch artist collective Atelier van Lieshout employ
standard industrial measurements to produce and create
series of modular objects and constructions, which offer
practical, adaptable solutions to everyday problems, focusing
entirely on the client and his desires. Behind modernity's
clarity and rationality, these objects and interiors offering
optimum physical comfort, are exercises in self-reliance and
self-provision; artifacts are intended to facilitate the survival
of the fittest. They are objects of personal obsession, buildings
and implements, which represent the materialization of hidden
but basic drives of society, such as eroticism and power.

opposite above Wim Delvoye, *Cloaca – New and Improved*, 2001
The Belgian artist Wim Delvoye has always been preoccupied
with materials of fabrication used in industrial design. The title
of his installation, *Cloaca*, means a cavity in the pelvic region
of most invertebrates, or a sewer. Delvoye created a perfect
reproduction of the human digestive tract. The machine was
fed three times a day in order to excrete once. The final product
was wrapped and sold as an edition with a certificate listing
the ingredients. The installation included a fully equipped
kitchen in which a sponsor provided food for the machine.
Delvoye plays with the balance between high and low culture,
the works are both highly crafted and functional, as well
as absurd.

above Sissel Tolaas, *It must be the weather, Part 1: Dirty 1*, 2001
The Norwegian artist Sissel Tolaas operates on the margins
of traditional perception. Her work appears in the guise of
experiments which use fire, water and air. By delving into the
world of the ephemeral, the artist explores the conventions
of space which are activated through the bodily experience
of the audience. Following a process of extensive research
in Deptford, London, which utilized sophisticated 'Headspace'
technology, a process developed by the perfume industry,
Tolaas was able to extract specific smells which prevailed
in the area. In collaboration with a Perfume House in Paris
she produced a perfume of the area entitled 'Dirty 1'. A video
accompanied the exhibition showing the view through a camera
attached to a dog exploring the area, while a soundtrack
provided local weather reports and recordings of the local
Salvation Army band.

right Lili Fischer, *Meute im Museum* (Mutiny in the Museum), 2001
In *Meute im Museum* the German artist Lili Fischer focused on concerns with natural phenomena, mediated through social role-play. Her work demands that viewers 'act on each other in a two way transfer of information'. In this installation, a transfer of identity took place between the animal characters and the audience, as visitors were asked to wear rat costumes to view the exhibition.

right Simone Michelin, *Bonjour Bonsoir Adieu Tristesse* (Good morning Goodnight Farewell Sadness) 2001
The installation of the Brazilian artist Simone Michelin was an interactive, three-dimensional structure. The system operated a jukebox, which was set in motion through a plug-in and -out telephone line. The participant could select between eight different sequences of video, featuring popular love songs and interviews recorded from public radio. An LCD (flat-screen) monitor displayed animated images of mouths, noses, eyes and tiny vulvas.

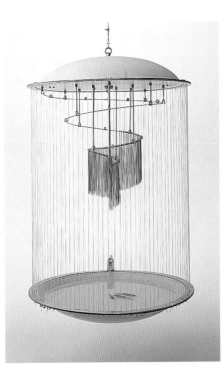

left Maywa Denki, *Uke-TEL (NAKI-U1)*, 1998
This installation consisted of a fish cage containing a special device. Hanging needles fell from the roof when the spectator dialed the telephone time signal. The fish swimming at the bottom was at risk from the falling needles.

below Jeroen Offerman, *Silent Boatman*, 2000
The installation by the Dutch artist Jeroen Offerman addressed questions of evidence and proof provided by the site. Paper casts of debris found on a dry riverbed functioned as a link between the original site and the gallery. The British artist Simon Moretti collaborated in the work, and added his own *Cover-Versions*, small felt copies of Offerman's casts.

above Jose Dávila, *Open Studio*, 2000
The Mexican artist's installations deconstruct architectural spaces. At Oxford in 2000, the artist's answer to the working site was to reconstruct his studio in the open air. Visitors coming to view new work were instead confronted with a makeshift studio in a field. No work was made in this space, but the artist led informal discussions on the nature and site of art production.

above Veronika Witte, *Institute for socio-aesthetic research (ISF)*, 2001–2002
This installation was a work in progress in times of genetic engineering. It presented a pseudo-scientific questionnaire about the image that visitors had of their body. Using multiple-choice questions and drawings of their ideal physical appearance, it confronted the viewers with fictitious possibilities of genetic manipulation.

above left and right Allan Wexler, *Vinyl Milford House*, 1994
The American artist constructed this piece too small to contain a bedroom, bathroom, kitchen and dining room all at once. The furniture and equipment necessary for these arrangements were stored in crates integrated into the four exterior walls. They bulged out, leaving the interior empty, but were pulled in when required. This project was a suburban backyard survival kit.

right Christian Jankowski, *Mein erstes Buch: Inszeniertes Schreiben* (My First Book: Staged Writing), 1998
German artist Christian Jankowski created an exhibition consisting of six different installations which changed from week to week. Following the expert advice given by important publishers who were invited to meet the artist in the exhibition, the artist produced his first book.

below Renée Green, *Between and Including Partially Buried in 3 Parts*, 1999
The American artist Renée Green's work poses questions on the nature of art production. Through her pieces, she demonstrates how work and leisure activities cross between different cultural domains. Green's work is interactive, combining video-lounges with films, soundworks and web pages, enabling the audience to use it for the purpose of social interaction, or simply as a means of gathering information.

right Ana Miguel, *I love you*, 2000
In this work the Brazilian artist Ana Miguel used knitted fabrics, velvets and silk to create a bed on the gallery floor for visitors to lie on and rest their head on the heart-shaped pillows. The visitor relaxed beneath a series of spider webs containing teeth and a love song soundtrack was triggered by the weight of the head on the pillow. Miguel's work lures the visitor into a trap of ambiguity, leaving the audience unsure whether the experience is pleasurable or sinister.

below Simon Moretti, *A Space for Conversation*, 2000
The installation by the London-based artist consisted of five circular carpets placed in the Turbine Hall of Tate Modern, London. A simple communication exercise ensued among the museum public. They were given a pen and a piece of paper and asked to communicate without spoken language, only through drawings. They engaged in a process of negotiation, which generated a number of images produced collaboratively.

above Muntean/Rosenblum, *Where else*, 2000
The Austrian artist Markus Muntean and the Israeli artist Adi Rosenblum have collaborated since 1992. In *Where else* they transformed the gallery of the Vienna Secession into a generic, non-functional cafeteria. Elevator music was piped into the room and a series of urban youth portraits hung on the walls. The images were derived from popular culture magazines. On the opening night live performers in colour-coordinated outfits posed motionless as cleaners. The performance was videoed and replayed throughout the duration of the exhibition.

left Jiri Kratochvil, *Joseph*, 1998
The Czech artist Jiri Kratchovil's installation, *Joseph*, was based on a mathematical formula. The display contained fish tanks and movement sensors connected to a bank of computers which monitored the passage of the fish between the three different coloured, interconnected aquaria. A soundtrack was also generated by the activity of the monitoring devices. His investigation into neurology and psychiatry and the effects of electromagnetic radiation on living cells, led to the 'Hive', a construct used by both scientists and appropriated by artists through history.

time and narrative

Despite yourself...you're impressed by the fact that you're going to completely disappear.

In a rapidly changing world, time and memory are key concerns for contemporary artists. Though borrowing from existing methodologies, artists depart from personal experience to construct their own spaces of memory. The singular term 'history' is under constant threat from the emergence of multiple 'histories'. Many artists have shied away from commenting on grand narratives, preferring to focus on the story of the everyday. They have used this concern with memory by focusing on official and unofficial means of retrieval, in an attempt to question existing systems through more private and individual means.

The exhibition 'Deep Storage – Collecting, Storing, and Archiving in Art' (held in Munich, Berlin and Düsseldorf, and subsequently at P.S.1 Contemporary Art Centre, New York, and at the Henry Art Gallery, Seattle, 1998) concerned itself with an examination of memory. It brought together a wide range of artists and works on the theme of archive and storage, a concern usually confined to museum specialists.

One of the key exhibitors in 'Deep Storage' was the German artist Karsten Bott. His project, *Archive of Contemporary History*, is an archive in progress, which has been growing for well over ten years, and contains thousands of everyday objects. A selection is displayed at each site and new objects are added to the collection. When constructing installations such as *One of Each* (2001), the artist chooses objects for temporary display from this vast archive and lays them out in specific configurations. Visitors are prevented from touching the items, as they can only view the exhibition from a raised walkway straddling the space. Once the installations are dismantled, all the objects are carefully wrapped and placed in cardboard banana boxes. Duly catalogued, they are stored on racks in a room dedicated to the collection. This room provides a second site, but one to which neither curators nor audiences have access. The artist has thus appropriated archival strategies, while dealing literally with 'rubbish'. He has turned collector, affording himself the privilege of the museum: to gather, catalogue and selectively display.

Such displays owe a debt to the celebrated works of the art historian Aby Warburg, *Mnemosyne Atlas*, and the theorist Walter Benjamin, *Arcades Project*. Though different, both are linked by a concentration on archiving knowledge and the philosophical readings to which they lend themselves. As the critic Geoffrey Batchen writes in the catalogue for 'Deep Storage', 'Exchange rather than storage has become the archivist's principal function, a shift in orientation that is evidenced in the flurry of networked projects that are under way all around the world.'

The theme of exchange forms the basis for the installation *I feel better now, I feel the same way* (1996) by the American artist David Bunn, who uses the discarded card catalogue of the Los Angeles Central Library, which was replaced by an electronic database. Bunn includes the archive in his work to create a poetic narrative from the endless readings provided by the display of the cards themselves. 'The artist as archivist' might be an appropriate way of describing the activity of the French artist Christian Boltanski. His incessant scavenging and collecting has resulted in displays of encyclopaedic proportions. In *Les Abonnés du Téléphone* (2000), Boltanski displayed thousands of international telephone directories which visitors were invited to browse, while a soundtrack played the list of twelve thousand registered voters living within a ten-minute radius of the gallery.

Boltanski's activities find an echo in the philosopher Vilém Flusser's assertion that we live in a society of recycling. By this he means that our lives are punctuated by objects, feelings and ideas that are endlessly retrieved and re-used. He thus aligns commercial waste recycling with psychoanalysis, both activities that aim to regenerate and to rebuild by sifting through and reinstating discarded and forgotten material. A number of artists have turned to personal recollections and anxieties as material for public displays. The British artists Bob & Roberta Smith, Mike Nelson and the French duo Loriot/Mélia

have all, in different ways, produced this kind of work, in which Installation becomes a means of gathering objects that evoke personal feelings and ideas to be displayed alongside one another. Loriot/Mélia's fragile reflections are arrangements made from broken toys, glass and plastic shards, a world of pathetic cast-offs. Bob & Roberta Smith's *Paint it Orange* (1997) was based on a childhood memory in which the artist's mother decided to use orange paint on all the furniture. The action was reprised in the gallery which was filled with the adult artist's various belongings, including his car, all of which were painted in the same luminous colour. Mike Nelson creates atmospheric installations in interlocking rooms, sparsely filled with objects from his own storerooms. These claustrophobic spaces give an impression of recent abandonment and melancholy. Such works are not archives in the institutional sense, nor do artists who use archiving methods aim to parody them. It is the emphasis on personal narratives that marks such work, the narrative of objects that have deep, personal associations. Individual memory is thus turned into a disrupted and discontinuous archive of history. Contemporary culture is so saturated with the idea of its historical authenticity that it has become fascinated with endless speculative re-interpretations of episodes in the near or distant past. Subjecting history to constant analysis and counter-analysis has contributed to a mistrust of any unifying historical explanation governing issues of identity, politics and culture and to a mistrust of any value systems which provide clear frameworks for moral or aesthetic judgment. Instead, each object, each experience, each incident, each image must be evaluated according to its own particularities and itself constitutes evidence, so that the image becomes as real as the event it portrays. 'There is no higher order of experience or material form that aesthetic practice can offer or separate cultural space in which it can dominate. The real,' states the theorist Peter Osborne, 'now coincides with its image'. The conflation of the real with its images provides the central argument in the installation *Garden* (2000) by the British artist Marc Quinn, which featured a large glass tank containing a flower garden. The plants were real and were prevented from wilting by the temperature-controlled formaldehyde in which they were immersed. Taken from their original context, they were preserved in the exhibition in what appears as 'archival suspension'. Drawing on the ideas of the French philosopher Michel Foucault, art historian Irit Rogoff writes that 'accentuating the performative aspect of the archive has allowed us to move away from solid sites of accumulated knowledge to a series of "archive effects".' While we may understand archives as a 'technology of control', it has also given rise to 'the perception of archives as the construction site of fantasmatic fictions.'

The work of Jane and Louise Wilson might be viewed in this context. Their video installation *Stasi City* (1997) was made in a former East German secret service headquarters. The secret police files once represented the dream of the perfect record of a nation's private activities and, as such, provided fertile ground for the artists' video works. 'We became focused on the meaning embedded in buildings, that certain sites represented,' the artists stated. And yet, the installation did not seek to reveal hidden historical truths; instead, the spaces served as memory triggers for the audience to imagine what remains invisible. The techniques employed by Jane and Louise Wilson are closely related to developments in current film-making, in which the image has become progressively unstable and unreliable. 'Cinematographic and videographic techniques – the artisanal invention of dissolves, feedback, slow-motion and time-lapse, zoom, live and decayed broadcast – now appear to have been premonitory signs, symptoms of a de-realisation of sensory appearances,' writes the theorist Paul Virilio. Location as such has disappeared, since our traditional visual link with place has been broken. The separation between location and viewer is due precisely to the acceleration of contemporary living and the establishment of tele-technologies. Virilio's position is borne out by the contemporary practice of Installation art in which the certainty of location is replaced by the restlessness of the artist and viewer. However, the

Mike Nelson, *The Coral Reef*, 2000
British artist Mike Nelson creates labyrinthine, large-scale architectural installations. *The Coral Reef* was a collection of shabby and disquietingly vacant reception rooms where viewing became an act of storytelling as the spectator picked a way through the curious amalgam of identities and histories. Nelson fuses encyclopaedic, though idiosyncratic references – which are often defined through the irony and kitsch of his materials – into three-dimensional narratives.

continuing popularity of projects based on personal memory, dependent on the artist's ability to recombine familiar elements in unusual ways, points to the need for private worlds with their own logic. In these, the artist's imagination provides stability and purpose.

The pursuit of memory through archival techniques is invariably a melancholic activity. The current fascination with archives for artists represents a desire to internalize and divert the narrative, rather than a need to critique such structures employing its own methods. It is the 'archival effect', as Rogoff argued earlier, that remains the key for the artist, along with an engagement with the 'slowness' and introspection of such an activity in which the work searches for its own boundaries. The French philosopher Jean-François Lyotard explains:

A Postmodern artist or writer is in the position of a philosopher: the text he writes, the work he produces is not in principle governed by pre-established rules. (These) rules and categories are what the work of art itself is looking for. The artist or writer, then, is working without rules in order to formulate the rules of what will have been done. Hence, the fact that work and text have the characters of event.

In this way, artists working with the retrieval of memory through found or invented narratives, are creating 'events' in which the work searches for its own context and boundaries; it is time itself that is revealed and experienced as the central subject. Since all narratives reference time, the artist uses these techniques to remind the viewer of their own story and experience of time.

right Jane and Louise Wilson, *Stasi City*, 1997
The images were projected simultaneously on four screens in the gallery, depicting a journey around abandoned secret service intelligence headquarters in East Berlin. Long corridors with identical offices, desolate spaces and decontamination chambers were revealed. The work was not explicitly political, rather it was concerned with powerlessness and horror. A soundtrack of static interference and clanking added to the drama and the twin artists were filmed keeping guard. This repetitive mirroring and doubling occurred throughout this installation, as well as in other works by the British artists.

right David Bunn, *I feel better now, I feel the same way*, 1996
As libraries replace their card catalogues with on-line databases, the cards themselves, obsolete, bulky and worn, are usually thrown away. For his work, the American artist David Bunn rescued two million cards from the Los Angeles Central Library. Using them as raw material, he directed the viewer's attention to the poetic trace. The work returned the obsolete artifact to the world as a living archive of reverie.

below Christian Boltanski, *Les Abonnés du Téléphone* (The Telephone Subscribers), 2000
Christian Boltanski transformed the exhibition space into a library of three thousand telephone directories from around the world. Spectators were invited to look through them and scan for familiar names. The exhibition included a specially commissioned sound piece in which the names of twelve thousand registered voters living within a ten-minute radius from the gallery were read out from different points. This archive of the whole world in the gallery space was fundamentally flawed and incomplete. Over the past four decades, Boltanski has explored archiving and the loss of the individual identity in the midst of collective experience and memory.

above Amanda Wilson, *Mirror*, 1997
Conceived as part of the 'Mirror' exhibition in 1997, the work of the British artist Amanda Wilson returned the viewer's attention to an investigation on the construction of individuality. In the basement of the space she constructed a series of wooden, backlit vitrines, which contained traces taken from her newborn child.

left Teresa Serrano *Vanishing City*, 2001
Small cacti gardens were placed inside three 'stroller' suitcases in the Programa gallery in Mexico City. Audiences were invited to move at will within the gallery space.

opposite below Darren Almond, *H.M.P. Pentonville*, 1997
Almond's work addresses concerns with duration and time. *H.M.P. Pentonville* was a live broadcast of limited duration. Television cameras relayed the interior of a deserted cell in Pentonville Prison, London, to the Institute of Contemporary Art, London, in real time. The tiny cell was projected onto the gallery wall, oppressive and bleak. Almond wanted to picture a space impossible to imagine, dead and inert, sparse and institutional. Nothing moved or changed, except time and sound. In the frame, the video digital counter rattled through the seconds, while the incidental acoustics of the prison were amplified to an unbearable degree.

Maurizio Cattelan
below left *Lift*, 2001
below right *Lift*, 2001 (detail)
Cattelan always incorporates a sense of the absurd and humour in his work. Punchlines of laconic narratives suspend story endings, as he deliberately shows the spectator only a clue or an out-of-context iconic figure. He describes his work in relation to theatre, for 'theatre, like art, is a biological function. It's just like everyday, every minute'. Life-size and miniature scenes are presented in which Cattelan is both director and character in his schizophrenic reality. His purpose is to dethrone authority and to play with the notion that in his world, art is condemned to tell untruths while maintaining its sense of the ironic.

left David Allen, *Thames Piece*, 2001
On entering the basement of the
exhibition space, visitors of the
project *Thames Piece* were exposed
to underwater sounds. These were
transmitted live through a hydra
microphone in the nearby river Thames,
and relayed via an antenna, through
two mobile telephones.

right David Davies *Row 01*, 2001
The British artist David Davies researched the precise schedule of ongoing state executions in the USA and tracked the population on Death Row. *Row 01* relayed information concerning all significant decisions related to appeals, stays, commutation and the execution itself, onto an LED messaging system installed in the rear room of the space. At the start of the year there were over 3,700 prisoners waiting on Death Row.

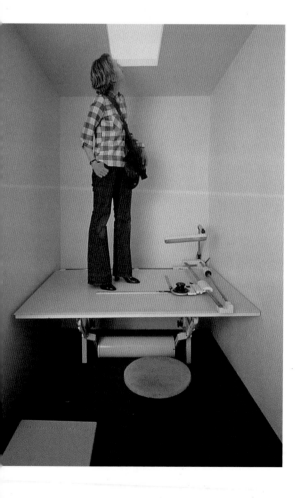

left Massimo Bartolini, *Zwei Horizonte (particolare)*, (Two Horizons, detail), 2002
The work of the Italian artist Massimo Bartolini deals with the effects of light and space and is filled with visual boundaries and illusions. This piece plays with an experience, both visual and corporeal, which is shared by the viewer. The installation for Manifesta 4 consisted of a series of domestic rooms bathed in intense light. Visitors entered one of the rooms, climbed on top of a drawing table and put their heads through a trapdoor in the ceiling. A recurring motif in his work is the spectator's ability to observe, while being denied access to proceed.

opposite below 'Archive', *Group Exhibition*, 1995
The exhibition 'Archive', 1995, coincided with the Museum of Installation's move to another location in London, and represented five years of projects. Conceived and designed by the organization's curators, in association with architects Simon Miller and Alain Chiaradia, it featured over thirty artists who were asked to exhibit works, prepared and previously shown at the Museum of Installation, as archive versions. In addition, all other parts of the museum were systematically catalogued and displayed, including its entire office and contents, as well as the walls of the space. The show represented an attempt to present a living and interactive archive of Installation art.

left Juan Cruz, *Driving Back*, 1999–2000
This sound installation featured two loudspeakers in an empty gallery space. A resonating soundtrack of the artist related a car journey into the countryside. As the topographical details accumulated, a mental map formed in the listener's mind. *Driving Back* presented Cruz's own account as a mediated process of communication. First, it was a recollection, filtered through the artist's memory; next, it was performed, with diversionary rhetoric and idiosyncratic tangents; and finally, it was presented to the listeners, who created yet another layer of meaning through their own memories of similar excursions.

above Jason Rhoades, *The Great Sea Battles of Wilhelm*, 1994–95

The assemblage artworks of the American artist Jason Rhoades are random collections which, though arranged with great deliberation, have gone beyond control. His work deliberately accumulates trash of everyday consumerism, found objects or items, some of which are still in their packaging, creating visual archives out of the reminders of the sites of everyday life. Picking up on biographical data *The Great Sea Battles of Wilhelm* recreated a fictional portrait of a collector's life. Beyond the biographical frame of reference, the installation followed an intuitive and imaginary concept derived from the artist's idea of life on the move – most spectacularly suggested through the giant suitcase structure that housed the piece.

right Tracey Emin, *My Bed*, 1998
The British artist Tracey Emin exhibited *My Bed* unmade and rumpled after a week's illness, complete with all the paraphernalia she had used in it, books, bottles, cigarette butts, condoms and handkerchiefs. In an era of superficiality, this private and autobiographical emblem of the artist's everyday life was exhibited as an authentic statement about herself and her relationships.

below Liza Lou, *Trailer*, 1999–2000
Liza Lou's dazzling beaded tableaux transform the most familiar settings of American domestic life into exuberant spectacles. At the same time, by hand-stringing the millions of tiny glass beads which go into such scenes as this, the artist describes the labour-intensive activity as elevating, repetitive 'women's work', almost a form of meditation.

above Ann Hamilton, *Mattering*, 1997
An undulating canopy of red-orange silk divided the gallery space in half laterally and visitors shared the territory with five male peacocks. Barely audible were the recorded sounds of an opera singer giving lessons to a student – and of the student mimicking the teacher. A wooden pole rose through a large circular hole in the silk and a figure sitting on a seat attached to the pole drew an endless thin blue line from a small white porcelain ink-pot on the ground, wrapping the inked ribbon around one hand until it formed a dense ball. The binding was then cut and dropped to the floor, only for the process to begin anew.

opposite below left David Wilkinson, *Untitled*, 1999
A rotating projector showed a forty-five-second film loop. The progress of the image around a cylindrical screen was synchronized to follow a 360-degree camera pan, filmed in the nearby Charlton Park, where, thirty years earlier, Antonioni shot scenes for the film *Blow Up* (1966).

opposite below right David Wilkinson, *Untitled*, 1996
The beam from a video projector was split through a system of mirrors to cover the surface of a latex weather balloon suspended from the gallery ceiling.

right Dermot O'Brien, *Untitled*, 1995
The installation by the artist Dermot O'Brien dealt with language and its sensory support structures. A pattern of small, coloured air fresheners installed on the wall of the gallery, made reference to written language which remained indecipherable to the sighted but was 'visibly' encoded in braille for the blind. The powerful and sweet smells overwhelmed the space. The discs provided the audience with an olfactory reference to these sample smells, which are usually employed to mask noxious household odours.

left Sam Taylor Wood, *Third Party*, 1999
Seven films were shot simultaneously on seven motor drive
cameras, a deliberate use of multiple images to deconstruct
traditional film techniques. Over ten minutes, this process
broke down the usual chronological sequences of film.
In *Third Party* the London-based artist Sam Taylor-Wood
directed each projection as a finite, unedited sequence of
its own. The cameras shot whatever was in front of them.
As a theme, the party is a much used motif in cinema. From
Antonioni and Warhol to Kubrick, they are places of alienation,
seduction and jealousy, places for quick sex, oblivion and
unexpected encounters, places of intoxication, light and
darkness; places of endless tedium. While choosing a familiar
theme, Taylor-Wood unsettles the audience through her
narratives and unconventional cinematographic techniques.

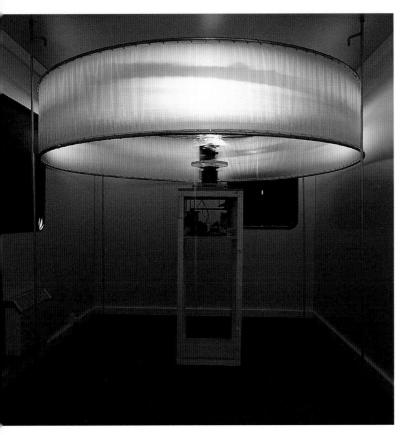

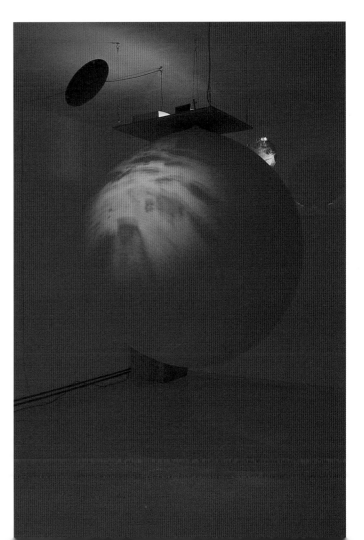

right and below Damien Hirst, *Love Lost (Large River Fish)*, 2000
Hirst's preoccupation with dissecting animals, revealing their insides and suspending them in formaldehyde, challenges the ideas of inertia and beauty. Within this theme of preserving and freezing motion, the work of the British artist is extended to the play with animate and inanimate objects. He used the form of the enclosed space to capture objects in a large museum vitrine for this work, creating an estranged and claustrophobic environment from which the viewer was excluded.

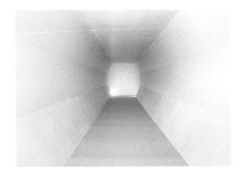

left Phyllida Barlow, *Depot*, 1995
This work by the British artist Phyllida Barlow related to the gallery as a storage space of lost or forgotten objects and referred to a state of incompleteness and dislocation. Large timber structures were brought together with pliable shapes, which were placed near or attached to them. This created a narrative of remaking and appropriating the originals, which then only functioned as bad copies.

below Mona Hatoum, *Homebound*, 2000
A sparse, 1950s living room and bedroom was dimly lit and fenced off by cables, reminiscent of high-security borders. Kitchen utensils were distributed across the furniture and wired to each other and small light bulbs glowed intermittently. The Lebanon-born artist experimented with the alienation of everyday objects, in order to speak of her ambivalent relationship to home and family.

above Knut Åsdam, *Psychasthenia (5)*, 1998
Working with the 19th-century notion of Heterotopias, Utopian Sites, The Norwegian artist Knut Åsdam writes that 'Cinematic space is a notion of space as narrative, a space as an unfolding of a certain idea of the unconscious'. In this sense he is more interested in looking at and working with space as a 'temporality of unfolding intensities...of different velocities; so it becomes a space of velocity, a space in which to fall in love, have adventures or dream.' This is, however, the space in which people experience restriction, suppression or defeat – a political space, which is also one of fantasy and memory.

below Alexander Brodsky, *Coma*, 2000–2001,
For *Coma*, the Russian artist Alex Brodsky created a miniature city of houses and skyscrapers made of clay and attached to intravenous feeding tubes, which nourished the town with a continuous drip of crude oil. His evocative work reflects the idea of a society that has stopped believing in progress and has been captured in a coma-like state of ghostly inertia.

opposite below Marc Quinn, *Garden*, 2000
Garden was described as a kind of homage to the 16th-century artist Hans Holbein. Impressed by Dutch art of the period and its preoccupation with the representation of nature and the human figure, Quinn commented: 'it's like the last judgement of the vegetable world'. A perfect image of eternity was provided by the display of flowers, frozen in silicon oil, controlled at a temperature of -20°C. The artist's main preoccupation was with the process of prolonging the lives of plants in an attempt to freeze and immortalize time and beauty.

right Hans Op de Beeck, *Border*, 2001
The spectator enters a vast, darkened room in which a moving image of a small group of people in a confined and abstract space is projected onto one wall. Their strange, whispered, but strongly amplified conversation, is hard to situate, but intriguing. Gradually, the group is surrounded by a life-size, X-ray image of a loaded truck and it becomes clear that these people, refugees, are locked in a box in the depths of a cargo lorry. Their conversation takes on another meaning.

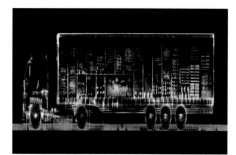

left Hans Op de Beeck, *Location I*, 1998 The Belgian artist's scale model of crossroads in a deserted landscape, deliberately set up at shoulder height, was installed in a darkened space illuminated with blue light simulating night time. Op de Beeck's miniaturized replicas of anonymous public spaces make the spectators feel as though they are inside the models, a moment shared between the artist and the audience. These still and quiet places, which represent a kind of timeless nowhere, carry an atmospheric mood without offering any story.

opposite Tadashi Kawamata, *Les Chaises de traverse* (The Shortcut Chairs), 1998
A double installation by the Japanese artist Kawamata connected two buildings of important historical significance – the Synagogue in Delme and the Hôtel Saint-Livier in Metz, France. Kawamata decided to reuse two thousand old chairs and erected a vertical structure into an imposing wall in the yard in Metz. This corresponded to the height of all the chairs laid out horizontally, separating the two floors in the Delme Synagogue. The artist also placed single chairs next to the plastic seating in thirty bus shelters along the route between Metz and Delme. Kawamata is preoccupied with the concept of contemporary chaos theory and issues of urbanism. He also chooses the locations of his works carefully, researching the city, collecting necessary materials and involving local communities.

below Rosemarie McGoldrick, *What Katy Did* in 'Day for Night', 1999
As part of the exhibition 'Day for Night' organized by the Museum of Installation, London, the British-born artist Rosemarie McGoldrick installed miniature cages in a Portacabin. The metal cages contained speakers which were connected to a computer programme. As listeners approached, the shrill sound of crickets was switched from one cage to another.

Loriot/Mélia
above *Le Leurre et l'agent du leurre*
(The Illusion and the Illusion's Agent), 1994
above left *Ready Made in China*, 2000
left *Le Diable Probablement* (Probably the Devil), 1993–2000
The French artists Loriot/Mélia create optical illusions and tricks of light to achieve cinematic images. Carefully sifted debris is used as material for the production of images which are caused by bouncing light through the meticulous arrangement of the debris. The original material appears as if removed from an archaeological dig, while the resulting images take the form of a cinematic light show. The concept of landscape was addressed in *Ready Made in China* which featured a spinning mountain range diorama, achieved by illuminating a bicycle wheel studded with glass shards. The illusion of a distant aeroplane, which appeared to be heading towards this mountain range, was glimpsed in an adjacent work. The resulting overall panorama triggered the memory of a classic cinematic moment where the plane either crashes into the rock or disappears into the distance.

above Bob & Roberta Smith, *Paint it Orange*, 1997
Paint it Orange was based on an autobiographical event of the
British artist Bob & Roberta Smith. As the artist's mother
painted items of furniture with a coat of bright orange gloss,
she ruined a set of Windsor chairs and devalued her son's
bicycle. Smith recalls: 'As a five year old I was instantly taught
how art could liberate and emancipate whilst also destroying
and humiliating.' The work points to sincerity through failure,
to a genuine, obsessional desire to make something, eventually
leading to misconstrued notions of value or usefulness.

below Sarah Lucas, *Chuffing Away to Oblivion*, 1999
The British artist Sarah Lucas is known for her large-scale collages consisting of photocopies and cuttings from newspaper articles. The artist creates claustrophobic environments, which communicate an often aggressive directness in her handling of themes, such as sexism or violence through abstruse or outrageous images, as in this installation.

above and opposite page João Penalva, *From R.*, 2001
The Portuguese artist João Penalva transformed the Palazzo Vendramin in Venice into a sequence of improvised theatres, archival displays, video projections, photographs and vitrines.

Throughout the installation *From R.*, the audience was confronted with competition scenarios acted out on video and through sound. The Eurovision Song Contest contrasted with a conversation in Esperanto in which a couple failed to understand each other. Penalva

juxtaposed winning and losing with the fallibility of human nature and its susceptibility. The context and setting of the work within the Biennale commented on its competitive agenda.

opposite below Markus Wirthmann, *The Twentieth Century. Chapter V: The Total Eclipse*, 2000
The beam of a theatre headlight hit a turning mirror ball installed in the centre of the room, which cast a shadow on the wall opposite the headlight. The movement of the video camera enabled the apparent passage of the moon's shadow across the viewer's field of vision, and at the same time, the simulation of a total solar eclipse could be observed on a monitor. Simulating the telematic experience of a natural phenomenon, this work by the German artist challenged the clichés of the Western perception of the 'dark continent', ironically negotiating issues of Afro-centrism.

above Miquel Angel Ríos, *Si me buscas...no me encuentras* (If you look for me, you will not find me), 2001
This work by the Argentinian artist Miguel Angel Ríos was a three-screen piece depicting the artist's journey through the desert. The synchronized projections showed the artist collecting hallucinogenic plants available in the location. His experience was altered by the effect of the powerful drug, resulting in a series of surreal visions.

left Jeremy Wood, *The Map of Hope and Other Improbable Locations*, 2002
The British artist Jeremy Wood plays with and modifies existing artistic strategies. For this installation, Wood arranged furniture and lighting in a room, taking as reference original archival photographs of its 1960s interior. Visitors were invited to spend time in this retitled *Waiting Room*, either to wait indefinitely or to watch a short film essay, compiled from the application of Fluxist games of chance to the artist's own home-video footage. An exterior projection window was also set up for the theatre building showing an animation loop derived from Piet Mondrian's *Broadway Boogie-Woogie* (1942–43). This pseudo-advert would 'hopefully' catch the eye of people on the train passing in front of the theatre.

left Joe Banks, *Soundproofs*, 1998
In his work for *Soundproofs* the British sound artist Joe Banks used the live frequency of the national electricity grid. The resulting compression of sound was amplified through a series of sensitive nodes and produced a loud tremor, which vibrated throughout the building.

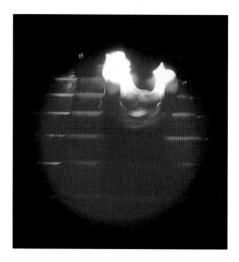

left Diana Thater, *Broken Circle*, 1997
The work of the Californian artist Diana
Thater avoids the comparison with
cinema, deliberately ignoring the
possibilities of technical perfection.
Her coloured projections bleed over
the walls and the images look as if
they have been projected on top of
each other. Her large-scale, overlapping
projections juxtapose images portraying
animal behaviour in man-made parks
and zoos. Her intention is to show that
both of them have been artificially
appropriated by mass culture.

opposite above right A. K. Dolven, *Stairs*, 2002
The work of the Norwegian artist A. K. Dolven deals with stillness, whether in her paintings or her video installations. In her films, actions are slow and deliberate and the camera often records the precise duration of a movement. As in *Stairs*, time is measured in relation to the unfolding of everyday processes.

Eija-Liisa Ahtila
above *Anne, Aki and God*, 1998
opposite below *Tuuli/The Wind*, 2002
The three-screen DVD installation entitled *Tuuli/The Wind* by the Finnish artist Eija-Liisa Ahtila charted a woman's deteriorating grip on reality as she fell prey to psychosis. A violent wind entered the room, leading the woman to turn her apartment upside down,

breaking furniture and destroying objects. This gradual mental breakdown was paralleled by the intricate and fluid choreography of the projection. Simultaneous yet different views of the apartment and a disrupted flow of linear time, along with the de-synchronization of events, contributed to the eventual dismantling of the familiar logic of screen narration.

this page Michael Petry, *Contagion*, 2000
Blood-red, hand-blown, human-heart-sized shapes hung from the gallery's ceiling in this work by the American artist Michael Petry. Each heart was suspended on steel wire at the height of the artist's heart, forming a large curved rectangle (modelled on the architecture of the room) which could be entered at any point and, like cell walls, the object was permeable. The gallery was floodlit with red light both day and night, but incoming sunlight meant that, slowly over the day and into the evening, the room dramatically changed colour. Petry had ascertained that the gallery was mainly visited at dusk (for theatre and cinematic performances) when the transition would be most obvious. Contagion was evocative of blood-related images, AIDS, hospitalization, transfusions, birth and death. As viewers approached the work they were suffused with red light, and appeared to other viewers as 'contaminated'. Once marked, as through a ritual, like blood brothers, they crossed over the threshold altered.

above Gabriel Kuri, *Momento de importancia* (Moment of Importance), 2001
This installation by the Mexican artist Gabriel Kuri adapts the temporality and significance of the event in which it is

below Catrin Otto, *Full House*, 1998
Using the traditional techniques of assemblage, collage and photomontage, Otto appropriates domestic plastic objects, which she reforms, remodels and then re-photographs from different angles. These photographs are cut out and reassembled among the original objects in the space. The suggestive play between the real and its photographic record immerses the viewer in a tactile environment. The artist's compulsive use of red and beige is employed as a metaphor for the visceral and corporeal illusions created by the work. The resulting effect is both obsessive and uncannily erotic.

exhibited. For this occasion, the piece served as a conference table for a talk about space and time, in which four academics and one cloud of cold steam participated. This confined the time the piece was on display to the duration of the talk.

left Teresita Fernández, *Bamboo Cinema*, 2001
American artist Teresita Fernández created this work from acid green poles arranged in a maze of concentric circles. As visitors walked between the poles, they experienced a flickering effect like the opening and closing of a camera shutter. The further viewers entered into the work, the greater became the effect of distortion of the surrounding landscape. The artist was concerned with the cinematic view arrived at by the movement and placement of the audience.

left Bodys Isek Kingelez, *Ville Fantôme* (Ghost Town), 1996
This self-taught Congolese artist constructs vibrant and meticulously ornate phantom cityscapes made out of paper and other materials. Models of corporate and public buildings in bright, flamboyant colours, hotels, stadiums, parliaments and other pieces of urban architecture, are integrated into a phantasmagoric and luxurious architecture of everyday travel and consumption. These 'architectonic simulations' place relationships of signs and representational systems under the command of a playful and utopian order of social, political and economic equilibrium of wealth. On the other hand, the artist presents a critique of the naïve and patronizing attitude of Western visionaries and planners towards the so-called 'primitive'.

opposite above right Daniel Guzmán,
Untitled, 2000
Guzmán creates highly idiosyncratic
space models using drawings which he
juxtaposes with found objects. He
also creates networks which connect
scattered objects, sounds, images and
activities. In *Prestano* (Loan, 1997), a
one-day show, Guzmán reconstructed
his sitting room in the exhibition space
and made several of his treasured
goods (books, records, videos) available
for the audience to borrow indefinitely.

below Karsten Bott, *Von Jedem Eins*
(One of Each), 2001
Since 1986, the German artist Karsten
Bott has obsessively collected,
categorized and documented objects of
life in the present, founding an 'Archive
of Daily Life'. His work consists of three
closely related areas: the archive, the
installations – which display selections
from the archive, such as this piece –
and films documenting people's lives,
traces and routines.

below Do-Ho Suh, *Seoul Home/L.A. Home/New York Home/Baltimore Home/London Home*, 1999
This piece hung from the ceiling like a spectre, swaying with the air currents in the space. Made from green silk, its transparency allowed light to shine through, creating the illusion that it not only floated, but also allowed the surrounding space to be reflected in the work. The Korean artist Do-Hoh Suh's installation was an exact replica of his childhood home in Seoul, and each time the work travelled to another city, the name of the host city was incorporated into the title. For Suh, this is a way of symbolizing his experience of transcultural travel. His work is a compelling statement on his identity and displacement.

Bill Viola, *Going Forth By Day*, 2002
opposite above *The Deluge*, panel 3
above *The Voyage*, panel 4
right *First Light*, panel 5
The work of American artist Bill Viola
investigates the tension between
stasis and motion, consciousness
and the unconscious. It is described
as an anachronistic 'suspension zone'.
These transient records of duration,
captured by monumental projections,
act as a series of metaphors for the
time in-between. *Going Forth By Day*
was a five-part projected digital-image
cycle which explored themes of human
existence: individuality, society, death
and rebirth. The five-image sequences
were synchronized on a continuous
loop and projected directly onto the
walls, giving the work the epic character
of moving frescoes. The story told by
each panel was embedded within the
larger narrative cycle.

the body of the audience

Western modernity since the nineteenth century has demanded that individuals define and shape themselves in terms of a capacity for 'paying attention', that is, for a disengagement from a broader field of attraction, whether visual or auditory, for the sake of isolating or focusing on a reduced number of stimuli.

Though audiences have come to expect a level of interaction and entertainment in Installation, other entirely different artistic strategies are emerging. The Mexican artist Carlos Amorales's event, *Funny 13* (2001), confronts the spectator with the figure of a 'devil'. The masked devil is dancing to disco music and attempts to entice the audience to participate; but the conventions of the gallery forbid it, making the spectator unsure about what action to take. Simply viewing might be seen as churlish, though dancing along might lay one open to ridicule. Caught between action and stasis, the viewer is effectively trapped. The trap is all the more effective because the viewers are lured towards a physical activity that promises pleasure. The ability to walk around the space occupied by the work and the possibility of close examination are no longer seen as being sufficient as an experience: the audience expects to play a significant part in the work, in its creation and reception. The artist's promise of participation, and its subsequent withdrawal, create anxiety in the audience. The work of the Spanish artist Santiago Sierra consists in paying groups of people to inhabit his creations. His subjects are often individuals, such as migrant workers, the unemployed or asylum seekers; some of his installations even involve voluntary incarcerations. However, he does not seek to expose the vulnerability of his collaborators, or turn them into performers, but instead focuses on the impotence of the observers, who are unable to alter the participants' predicament.

The work of the Italian artist Vanessa Beecroft has similar aims: tightly choreographed groups of photographic models, hired especially for the occasion and often naked, are displayed motionless in the gallery. Unlike Sierra's figures, Beecroft's models are at the other end of the social spectrum, their work glamorous, their bodies desirable. The photographic model here can be said to represent the ultimate simulation of a human being: it appears like one, yet its removal from everyday reality is absolute. Such installations have a finite timespan and, during their exhibition, no interaction from the public is welcomed. This lack of engagement is significant in the work and may be seen as its *raison d'être*. It would be natural for the public to wish to help the unfortunate asylum seekers, or to touch the beautiful models, yet it is their very proximity or palpability that renders them forbidding. The subjects, immensely real, remain achingly beyond the audience's grasp.

This position is confirmed by the art historian Jonathan Crary: 'Spectacle is not primarily concerned with a looking at images but rather with the construction of conditions that individuate, immobilise, and separate subjects, even within a world in which mobility and circulation are ubiquitous.' Moreover, as the viewer looks at the objects that make up the installation in a given space, a perspectival shift occurs. Whatever the spectator can see constitutes one point from which he could be seen. The mirroring between the viewer and the viewed becomes endless. The French psychoanalyst Jacques Lacan stated: 'I see myself seeing myself...I see outside, that perception is not in me...it is on the objects that it apprehends.' Lacan's statement pinpoints the predicament of the viewer: one cannot see without being aware of being seen. The desire for a secluded viewing experience is always accompanied by the self-conscious thrill of being caught in the act.

The video installations of the American artist Gary Hill aptly illustrate the point made by Lacan. *Viewer* (1996) shows a tableau of people engaged in looking. They are lined up side by side, but are entirely isolated and unaware of one another. Instead, their gaze is directed outside the frame, ahead of them. They are looking at us, the viewers, as we look at them. Here, the wall of the projection acts as a hinge

between two worlds; what intrigues and unsettles the viewer is the lack of engagement or identification usually found in the cinematic experience. Instead we are confronted with an endless mirroring between the individuals and ourselves. Installation challenges the aesthetics of frontality, that is, the paradigm of cinematic screen and monitor. This engagement with frontality is expressed in the relationship between viewer and artifact to the extent that the audience participates in the work by becoming fused with it. Here, what is important is not the audience's ability to circulate round the figure or an object, but, on the contrary, the challenge to spectatorship by focusing on the viewer's frozen immobility. It may be argued that such installations act like surfaces, endlessly returning our gaze, rendering viewer and viewed the same. Similarly, the authorship of the work passes from the artist to the viewer.

From the Renaissance onwards, the position of the 'I' is central to perspective, and is privileged above all others. The world then becomes a picture or object to be viewed from a single angle. Thus, perspective suggests that the world circulates around the eye of the observer. Gilles Deleuze argues that cinema provides the opportunity to disrupt our self-centered perception, by providing competing viewpoints. The moving image challenges a view of the world that is entirely arranged around each individual. The filmic installations of the British artist Tacita Dean serve to illustrate Deleuze's point. *Fernsehturm* (Television

Tower, 2001) shows a view from the observation deck of a television tower in Berlin. The camera appears to turn in a panoramic sweep, but it is the room that is turning slowly on its axis. The camera's viewpoint remains static, but the space provides the movement through its rotation. In *Fernsehturm* the world rotates around the individual spectator, eliminating the need for movement.

The works of the Canadian artist Stan Douglas also require a static viewer. Stillness is conducive to 'paying attention', as argued by Jonathan Crary. However, Douglas's film projections hide intricate spatial arrangements and camera settings. The apparent simplicity of his footage is only made possible because of complex sets specially built for the works. As in Dean's work, the position of the spectator is questioned: the viewer is seduced by the film, yet has difficulty in working out how the scene is shot. These artists' installations require patient and concentrated viewing.

Writing on films and panoramas, the American academic M. Christine Boyer asserts that 'we begin to be faced with the absent-minded viewer who is uncritical of conventionality yet slates any innovation since it changes the format of endless repetition.' The waning of the unique artwork comes about through processes of replication and repetition of images. Repetition has become ubiquitous in contemporary art; indeed, it has become an essential condition of production and reception. The filmic

installations of British artist Douglas Gordon disrupt the inertia generated by repetition in works such as *Twenty-Four Hour Psycho* (1993) which slowed the classic Alfred Hitchcock film down to occupy a whole day. The installation *Feature Film* (1998–99) showed the same director's *Vertigo* (1958), along with footage of Bernard Herrmann's celebrated soundtrack of the movie being conducted by James Conlon of the Paris Opera. The conductor's actions were projected onto an enormous screen while the music surrounded the viewer in a wall of sound. The spectator was literally immersed in sumptuous sound and vision and the public's critical distance is eroded by the spectacle, sweeping away the viewer's bodily resistance.

Stanley Kubrick's 1968 film *2001: A Space Odyssey* provides a final example of the viewer's predicament. In the culminating scene, the spacepod of the astronaut Bowman, played by Keir Dullea, is transferred from outer space to an interior. The dwelling has no windows but is lit by an opaque glass floor, an arrangement usually found in suspended ceilings in museums which filter sunlight: the museum space is turned upside down. This reference to the museum is important, since it turns everything within the space into an exhibit. As the

Carlos Amorales, *Funny 13*, 2001
The Mexican artist Carlos Amorales works between 'decors', static installations and 'performances', actions undertaken by himself and other collaborators. In 'Funny 13', 2001, Amorales was dressed as a masked devil and exhorted the public to dance with him.

character appears in the room, dressed in a red spacesuit, he is confronted with his alter ego, albeit as a much older man, who, in turn sees himself as an ancient bed-ridden figure facing a floating, black, stone wall. The film set combines the aesthetics of the museum, that is, the past, with the technology of the future through the spacepod. Furthermore, the viewer's attention is directed from one viewpoint to another in a linear progression, a technique also used in the 19th-century museum, in which the spectator's attention is handed from one character to another as in a relay-race. The progression of shifting viewpoints follows the ageing process towards death and rebirth.

In Jean Baudrillard's description of 'private telematics' the author explains that 'each person sees himself at the controls of a hypothetical machine, isolated in a position of perfect and remote sovereignty, at an infinite distance from his universe of origin. Which is to say, in the exact position of an astronaut in his capsule, in a state of weightlessness that necessitates a perpetual orbital flight and a speed sufficient to keep him from crashing back into his planet of origin.' In *2001: A Space Odyssey* the space-shuttle turns into the museum. The figure in the set replaces the viewer, who thus witnesses his own self in stages of progressive disintegration. The end of the viewer's journey is the realization of his own disappearance. The more we look, the less we see ourselves: the Empire of the Senses masks our own vanishing.

this page and opposite above Christoph Draeger, *Apocalypso Place*, 2000
For the past decade the Swiss artist Christoph Draeger has commented on and documented the sites of both natural and manufactured disasters. Draeger approaches the distressing subject matter through strategies such as the re-enacting of thrillers or action films. He creates photographs, video installations and complex gallery environments which replicate ruined sites, destroyed houses or burned trailer parks. All involve a resounding critique of the preponderance of mass-media coverage of catastrophic events.

right Aernout Mik, *Piñata*, 1999
Inside a small space a video projection
was purposefully staged at floor level,
allowing the spectator to participate
with the protagonists. Within a domestic
setting, the actors destroyed anything
and everything. The concern of the
Dutch artist Aernout Mik was to provide
a platform on which the body became
the situation or site, acting out a game
plan of interaction and passivity.

right Douglas Gordon, *Feature Film*, 1999
For his installation the British artist Douglas Gordon filmed the conductor James Conlon leading a performance of Bernhard Hermann's musical score for Alfred Hitchcock's film *Vertigo*. The conductor's movements were synchronized on screen with the soundtrack. The artist addressed issues of guilt and fear, exploring them through repetition, enlargement and slow motion. The memory of the classic film, which was screened separately from Gordon's, conflicted with the actuality and scale of the conductor's image.

below Terry Smith, *Marking Time*, 1999
The video work by British artist Terry Smith was developed in Rome and filmed in London, and focused on the time when Casanova was alive. It was projected onto the walls of the Ca Rezzonico Museum, Venice, before its temporary closure. One screen depicted a game of poker in progress, the second showed a portrait of a woman's face, and each of the screens was shot to resemble a Caravaggio painting. The voice-over narrative consisted of a man describing the rules of poker, and a second voice stood in for the audience, asking questions about what was represented.

left Eric Steensma, *Roadmovie*, 2002
The Dutch artist Eric Steensman uses computer-generated video projections which are transformed using the theatrical illusion called 'Pepper's Ghost'. In *Roadmovie* a sheet of glass was placed between a number of monitors and the space, creating the illusion of miniature figures. The protagonists in this magical environment walked around and interacted with actual toy cars and other objects, while appearing suspended in mid-air.

below Abigail Lane, *The Inspirator*, 2001
This playful work by the British Artist Abigail Lane features the surreal projection of a panda playing a trumpet in the depths of a forest. A poster declared, 'Her mind was a wilderness, her world a wasteland and then from nowhere he returned'. This whimsical and unexpected spirit smiled fleetingly before disappearing, leaving only the outline of a grin. Derived from her long-standing fascination with late-19th-century theatrical phenomena, such as seances, freak shows, circus and magic acts, Lane created a funhouse of absurd narratives.

left Eric Duyckaerts, *How to draw a square*, 1999
The Belgian artist Eric Duyckaerts has a background in both law and philosophy and his work contains a humorous play between art and pseudo-scholarly discourse. He is interested in the fusion of reality and fiction and uses the device of the lecture as an ironic critique of the authority invested in the speaker. In his video lectures he takes on the character of the professor or logician. Duyckaerts's works explore the rhetoric of experimentation and pedagogical discourse.

below Nicolas de Oliveira and Nicola Oxley, *Burg Weogaran Dyreby*, 1996–98
Based on Wheatstone's 19th-century stereoscope, this work examined the relationship between the space and the audience. Two identical viewing devices were set up opposite one another and viewers were encouraged to interact with them. The mirrored tables allowed viewers to transform their perception of the space, culminating in their own visible removal.

opposite below Santiago Sierra, *Trabajadores que no pueden ser pagados remunerados para permanecer en el interior de cajas de cartón* (Six workers who cannot be paid for sitting inside cardboard boxes), 2000
This Spanish artist's work deals with political and social comment and the gap between the 'first' and Third World. His work challenges issues of employment, health, nationality and social origin, examining different political and economic systems and their consequences for individuals. During the project, asylum seekers volunteered to sit in narrow cardboard boxes for four hours daily for the duration of the exhibition. The boxes were closed and hid the participants from the viewer's gaze. The invisible silent presence was a shocking reminder of the predicament of asylum seekers, who are powerless because of the official restrictions imposed by the state on their ability to work and travel.

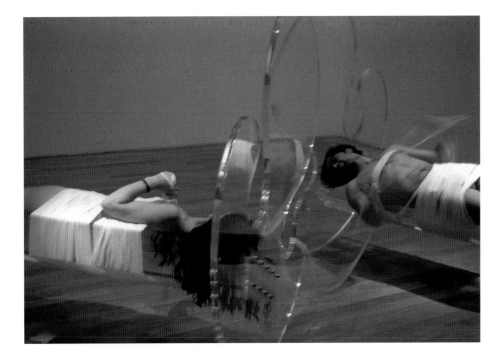

left Besnik and Flutura Haxhillari,
Die Gulliver Träumen (Gulliver's
Dreams), 1999
Besnik and Flutura Haxhillari's work is
concerned with their Albanian culture:
the constant upheavals of migration
have influenced the production of
pieces based on the literary figure
of Gulliver. Like Gulliver, the artists
are caught up in new contexts
and territories. The work is
autobiographical and acted out
with ironic humour, playing on the
estrangement and nostalgia of their
nomadic life.

opposite page Michael Landy, *Break Down*, 2001
Michael Landy's work explores aspects of contemporary
consumerism. Three years in the making, *Break Down* is the
British artist's most extreme project. He made an inventory
of his life, of everything that he owned: pieces of furniture,
records, articles of clothing, his car, books, gadgets and works
of art. Over five thousand individual items were drawn up and
catalogued. During a two-week period, Landy and his team
of workers, installed on public view in a disused department
store on London's Oxford Street, proceeded to systematically
number, dismantle and weigh every item. These were then
placed onto a specially constructed conveyor belt –

a production line of destruction. What was left at the end of
the elaborate process was powder, which the artists intends
to bury in a capsule under a shopping precinct. The only
physical evidence that survived the process was an artist's
book which acted like an inventory and included the
complete list of contents and an accessible public database.
Landy described the work as an audit of his life. He is
fascinated by the common currency of marketing information
which profiles and classifies individuals through 'data mining'.
Left with nothing, Landy escaped consumerism, only to admit
ironically that he is now the perfect person to sell to – the
ultimate consumer.

opposite Christine Hill, *Volksboutique Organizational Ventures*, 2002
The American artist Christine Hill dissects the institution of work, both in and outside the art context, appropriating daily influences to which an artist is constantly exposed. Hill portrays herself as living a variety of identities. She does not role-play, but performs in order to make a living, taking jobs that are often poorly paid and exploited (masseuse, shoeshine, striptease dancer). This project exhibited and sold the production of the work that took place in it, while attempting to create a space of discussion and a situation of exchange with the audience.

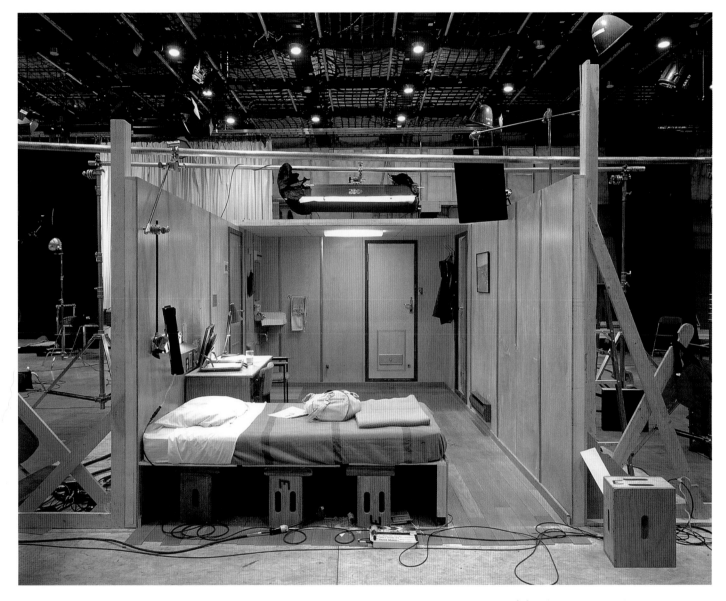

opposite and above Stan Douglas,
Journey into Fear: Pilot's Quarters 1 and 2, 2001
This work is based on two feature films of the same title,
one from 1942 and a 1975 remake. The Canadian artist
Stan Douglas recreated the setting of the films in which the
characters were cramped in an ocean container ship. While
the actions remained the same, the dialogue (co-scripted by
Douglas and Michael Turner) kept changing as it was dubbed
onto the endlessly revisited scenes. The piece lasted for over
six days, and was impossible to view in its entirety. In this work
the narrative chronology became a mathematical conundrum
of infinite possibilities, constantly dislodging the intricate plot.

right Olaf Nicolai, *Portrait of the Artist as a Weeping Narcissus*, 2000
The German artist Olaf Nicolai's sculpture depicts himself gazing at his reflection in a pool, in the manner of Oscar Wilde's Dorian Gray. Frozen in time, Nicolai's likeness sheds a tear.

opposite below John Bock, *Lombardi Bängli*, 1999
The German artist John Bock chooses the form of the lecture as his artistic medium. His aim is to transform simple structures and artistic tasks into abstract and absurd scenarios, which function as models of society. In his lectures, Bock combines language, dramatic elements and sculptural objects. He acts on 'stages' built from tables, cupboards or multilevel wood constructions. The objects are handmade or re-modelled accessories of the lecture, made out of clothing, electrical equipment, such as hoovers and mixers, or 'plastic diagrams' illustrating his mathematical explanations. After

the lecture, they are left on the stage to form 'theatrical collages'. The lectures are structured through different scenes in which Bock sometimes works with (non-professional) actors. Frequently he plays pop songs or classical pieces from a record player. The lectures are mostly recorded on video and later integrated into the installations.

below Christian Jankowski, *Rosa*, 2001
The artist's narrative video installations play a central role in his strategy of setting up complex scenarios around encounters with'normal', mundane behavioural patterns (supermarket shopping becomes a hunting expedition, the exhibition becomes a magician's act), transforming the ordinary into

filmic fantasies. Documentation and magic, reality and fiction can hardly be separated. He observes life as an open-ended set of adventures – which can have absurd consequences – and is narrator and observer, a commentator and prankster. Despite its hilarity, *Rosa* had a dark side, dwelling on the cruelty of seemingly normal situations. Set deliberately in the business world of art, the burlesque situations provided built-in-failure elements, although the bittersweet ending ultimately gave the spectator a feeling of redemption.

below Patrick Tuttofuoco, *Walkaround*, 2002
The Italian artist found inspiration for this work in a trip
to East Asia. The installation consists of a group of ten
skyscrapers made of wood, plastic, painted metal and neon
lights, each 6 feet tall and mirroring human scale. The high-
tech city centres with their Utopian architecture, hybrid forms
and atmosphere of futuristic kitsch were parodied in the work.
The constructions were like a children's building game, a
comment on how useless design can be when confronted
with an irrational and playfully anarchic vision.

opposite above Sylvie Fleury, *Bedroom Ensemble II*, 1998
The Swiss artist Sylvie Fleury has focused her art on the world
of fashion and consumerism, copying luxurious products and
developing branding techniques. *Bedroom Ensemble II*
stimulated the senses and created objects of desire as fetishes
of an affluent society. At the same time, the installation
criticized the cultural legacy left by them.

below Ana Laura Aláez, *Prostibulo* (Brothel), 1999
The Spanish artist Ana Laura Aláez confronts the viewer with
an interior resembling an oriental boudoir. In this profane
ambience the viewer was invited to act out their own fantasy.

THE BODY OF THE AUDIENCE

below and opposite above Hans Weigand, *Cotton*, 2001
Cotton is a combination by the Austrian artist Hans Weigand
of two structures built in the exhibition space. While one of
them shows video sequences of a modern version of the
Jerry Cotton story in the form of a photo-novel, the other
is an imitation of a design element from Stanley Kubrick's *2001:
A Space Odyssey*. The avant-garde Utopias of late-1960s design
in Kubrick's idealized sci-fi fantasy are combined with a story
steeped in the dime novel and pulp fiction.

left Roman Signer, *Kabine*, 1999
Much of the work of the Swiss artist
Roman Signer exists only as the trace
of an action. His materials are ordinary
and infused with practical experience,
yet in the context of his performances
they take on a life of their own, flowing
and forming responsive patterns. In
Kabine the artist exposed himself to an
explosion inside a specially constructed
shelter. The remains of the event
became part of the subsequent
exhibition. Signer describes his work
through a feeling 'for tragedy, for the
absurd, the senseless and the useless
that we humans inflict.'

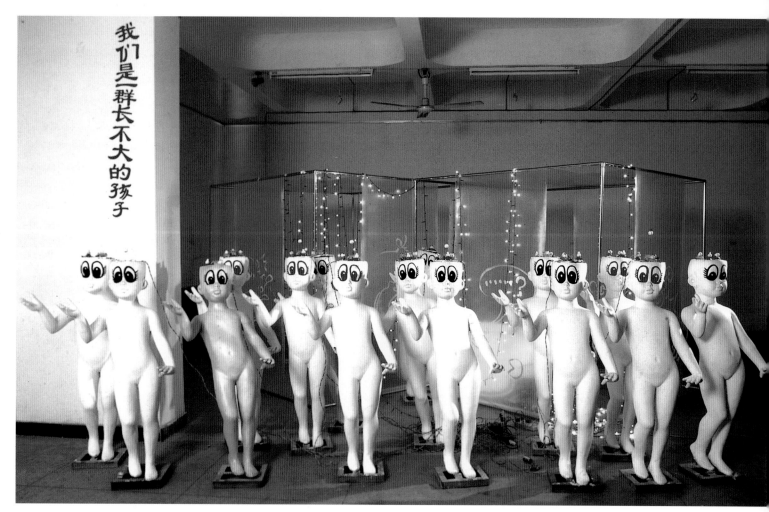

opposite above Patrick Tuttofuoco, *Velodream*, 2001
For Tuttofuoco's work, the SMAK galleries in Ghent, Belgium, were turned into a Velodrome. The exhibition featured a series of vehicles designed by the artist as portraits of his close friends which viewers were able to take for a spin. Tuttofuoco's work is concerned with play, entertainment, youth culture and sport.

opposite below Chinese Cartoon, *We Are the Kids Who Never Grow Up*, 2001
The work of the collaborative artists' group Chinese Cartoon takes its inspiration from the artificial world of computer animations, games and toys. In this installation the Chinese artist Huang Yihan refers to the conflict of the younger generation who remain physiologically immature in spite of being socially grown-up.

Charles Long and Stereolab
right *The Amorphous Body Study Centre*, 1995
right below Charles Long, *Holidays Situations*, 1999
The American artist Charles Long has collaborated with various artists and musicians to complete a series of complex pieces. *The Amorphous Body Study Centre* consists of a series of pod-like, organic forms with headsets for the viewer to listen to the songs of the British pop band Stereolab. It revealed the importance of the tangible in the emerging information-based reality.
For *Holidays Situations*, Long created a tableau of male and female mannequins in the window of the Saks Fifth Avenue store in New York. These acted as stand-ins for the viewer and posed in attitudes of fashionable boredom in opulent living rooms invaded by snow drifts. The work exuded humour, but masked a darker mood. One of the scenes referred to the claustrophobic landscapes of Stanley Kubrick's film *The Shining*. In another window, a snow globe, reminiscent of Orson Wells's *Citizen Kane*, was perched on a baroque foam structure. The tension between the mimetic shapes and posed figures was heightened by the electronic, upbeat mantra of the audio artist Mark Mothersbaugh, which included laughing, purring and ringing bells.

Mariko Mori, *Beginning of the End, Shibuya/Tokyo*, 1995
Mori's work presented a series of photographs showing her suspended in a plexiglas body capsule in urban public spaces all over the world. Mori believes in the necessity of Utopias, conveyed in works that are neither ironic nor naive. The implication is that we already live in a world where the machines are on the whole more colourful, lively and interesting than people.

right Mariko Mori, *Body Capsule*, 1995
The Japanese artist Mariko Mori celebrates herself as an art product, as a star born out of the world of image streams, who cleverly succeeds in mixing visions of fashion and architecture transforming them into virtual environments. She appears in her photographs dressed as a futuristic comic book figure or a sweet and harmless cyborg. For her work *Beginning of the End* (above), Mori encased herself in a Body Capsule to express a transcendence over space-time.

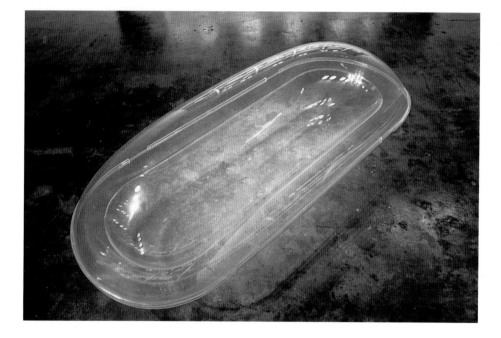

Thomas Eller, *THE Human Re-entering Nature*, 2000
The work of the German artist Thomas Eller responded
to the problems of the Japanese location in which it was
exhibited. Extreme seasonal conditions – an average of more
than two metres of snowfall in winter – and the pull of the big
cities, led to an increasing depopulation of the area. The artist
symbolically repopulated it with three figures mounted on
aluminium sheeting. These were covered in snow in the winter
and overrun with plants in the summer.

below Momoyo Torimitsu, *Miyata Jira*, 1997
The Japanese artist Momoyo Torimitsu describes her work as focusing on the tension between reality as perceived through the senses and physical or objectively real experience. The crawling robot *Miyata Jira* looked exactly like an ordinary Japanese businessman. Torimitsu, dressed as a nurse, assisted it as it crawled along the pavement. The work was a statement on the predicament of the Post-1960s economic boom, when individual identity became subsumed into a uniform collective. The artist takes general themes highlighted by Japanese culture and comments on the difficulties experienced when a society is so over stimulated by commerce and fantasy that common values and reality are overlooked.

above Vanessa Beecroft, *VB46.026.ali*, 2001
Since the mid-1990s the Italian artist Vanessa Beecroft has displayed a succession of scantily clad or naked women. All the women are made up and dressed in a similar way, resembling shopfront mannequin or models in fashion shoots. Standing before the public like living pictures, these set-ups are not performances; the figures do not move, they only take up a position. Neither the models, nor the public show any emotion and no comment is made. Derived from media images of commodified beauty, these ensembles suspend human communication, emasculating the charm of the erotic interplay.

Gary Hill, *Viewer*, 1996
Slightly larger-than-life colour images of seventeen labourers facing out from a neutral black background were projected onto a 45-foot-long wall. For this, five laser discs were synchronized so that the figures appeared to be standing side-by-side in a line. The men stood almost motionless, their movement limited to involuntary stirring – an incidental shifting from foot to foot, slight movements of the hands, and almost imperceptible changes in facial expression. There was no interaction among them, each man stood alone and gazed out from the plane of projection towards the viewer.

this page Tacita Dean, *Fernsehturm* (Television Tower), 2001
The British artist Tacita Dean's work is a 16-mm film made on location in Berlin, several hundred metres above ground level in the rotating room of the old East German television tower. Dean used the slow pan of the tower turning full circle as a metaphor for the reunification of Germany, a meeting of both cultures, old and new establishing a new world order.

notes on the text

Numbers in bold refer to pages on which quotations appear.

introduction

13 Michael Landy, *Breakdown*, exh. cat., London, 2001, p. 107.

13 Roberta Smith, 'Installation Art, a Bit of the Spoiled Brat', *New York Times*, 3 Jan. 1993.

14 Hal Foster, 'The Un/making of Sculpture' in Ferguson et al. (eds), *Richard Serra: Sculpture 1985–98*, Gottingen and Los Angeles, Calif., 1998.

14 Jean Baudrillard, *Simulacra and Simulation*, Ann Arbor, 1994.

15 Ilya Kabakov, *On the 'Total Installation'*, Ostfildern, 1995.

15 Rochelle Steiner (ed.), 'Spaces for Wonder', *Wonderland*, exh. cat., Saint Louis Art Museum, Miss., 2000, p. 36.

17 Robert Storr, 'No Stage, No Actors, But It's Theatre (and Art)', *New York Times*, 28 Nov. 1999.

18 M. Fried, 'Art and Objecthood', *Artforum*, Summer 1967. Quoted in Storr *op. cit.*

18 Steiner, *op. cit.*, p. 34.

22 Nicolas Bourriaud, *Postproduction*, New York, 2002, p. 12.

22 J. G. Ballard, interview by Lorenza Pignatti in *Tema Celeste*, 85, May/June 2001.

27 Neville Wakefield, 'The Passenger', *Frieze*, issue 67, May 2002.

28 Keith Tyson on *The News at Ten*, BBC, 28 October 2002.

28 Johanne Lamoureux, 'Exhibitionitis: A Contemporary Museum Ailment' in Chris Dercon (ed.), *Theatergarden Bestarium: The Garden as Theater as Museum*, London, 1990, p. 124.

29 Dieter Roelstraete, 'Sonsbeek 2001, A Place Odyssey' in Dieter Roelstraete (ed.), *Sonsbeek 9: Locus Focus*, Arnhem, 2001, p. 27.

29 Miwon Kwon, *One Place after Another*, Cambridge, Mass., 2002, p. 1.

30 Ilya Kabakov and Boris Groys, *Die Kunst der Installation*, Munich, 1996, p. 23.

30 Hal Foster, *The Return of the Real*, Cambridge, Mass., 1996.

30 Thomas Hirschhorn, *Contemporary Sculpture Projects Muenster*, Ostfildern-Ruit, 1997, p. 216.

31 James Meyer, 'The Functional Site', *Platzwechsel*, exh. cat., Kunsthalle Zurich, 1995, p. 29.

32 Kwon, *op. cit.*, p. 29.

32 Suzanne Lacy, *Mapping the Terrain: New Genre Public Art*, Seattle, Wash., 1995.

32 Walter Grasskamp, 'Art and the City' in K. Bussmann et al. (eds), *Contemporary Sculpture: Projects in Münster*, exh. cat., Ostfildern-Ruit, 1997, p. 10.

35 Oskar Bätschmann, *The Artist in the Modern World*, Cologne, 1997.

38 Michel Foucault, 'Of Other Spaces', in *Diacritics 1*, 16, Spring 1986. Quoted in *Politics, Poetics: Documenta X – The Book*, Ostfildern-Ruit, 1997, p. 265.

40 Nicholas Negroponte, *Being Digital*, London, 1996, p. 223.

42 Claire Colebrook, *Gilles Deleuze*, London 2002.

42 Colebrook, *op. cit.*, p. 100.

43 Sergiusz Michalski, *Public Monuments*, London, 1998.

44 Maria Lind, 'Learning From Art and Artists', in Gavin Wade (ed.), *Curating in the 21st Century*, Walsall, 2000, p. 94.

44 Hans Ulrich Obrist, in Gavin Wade (ed.), *Curating in the 21st Century*, Walsall, 2000, p. 54.

45 Richard Sennett, 'The Museum as an Anarchic Experience' in Chris Dercon (ed.), *Theatergarden Bestarium: The Garden as Theater as Museum*, London, 1990, p. 136.

47 Jeffrey Kastner, interview with Mary Jane Jacob, in *Public Art*, London, 1996.

47 Michael Landy, *Breakdown*, exh. cat., London, 2001, p. 109.

escape

49 Marc Augé, *Non-places: Introduction to an Anthropology of Super-modernity*, London and New York, 1995, p. 77.

49 Ina Blom, *Børre Sæthre*, exh. cat., Galleri Wang, Oslo, 2001.

49 Frederic Jameson, *Postmodernism, or, The Cultural Logic of Late Capitalism*, Durham, N.C., 1991, p. 87.

49 Paul Virilio, *Lost Dimension, Semiotext(e)*, New York, 1991, p. 35.

49 Sze Tsung Leong, 'Control Space' in R. Koolhaas et al. (eds), *Mutations*, Bordeaux, 2000, p. 187.

50 Jean-Pierre Bordaz, 'The World As It Should Be' in Idit Porat (ed.), *Absalon*, exh. cat., AFAA Tel Aviv Museum of Art, 1992.

50 Laurence Bosse, *Gregor Schneider*, exh. cat., Musée d'art Moderne de la Ville de Paris, 1998.

51 Jean Baudrillard, *Simulacra and Simulation*, Ann Arbor, 1994, p. 167.

51 Bernard Marcadé, 'Absalon's Monadology' in Idit Porat (ed.), *Absalon*, exh. cat., AFAA Tel Aviv Museum of Art, 1992.

51 'Biefer/Zgraggen' in H. Griese, E. Schmidt, (eds), *Do All Oceans Have Walls?* exh. cat., Künstlerhaus Bremen, 1998, p. 18.

51 J. Flam (ed.), *Robert Smithson, The Collected Writings*, Berkeley and Los Angeles, Calif., 1996

51 Aldo Bonomi, 'Smooth Space' in R. Koolhaas et al. (eds): *Mutations*, Bordeaux, 2000, p. 451.

53 Franz Kafka, 'The Burrow' in *Metamorphosis and Other Stories*, Harmondsworth, 1981, p. 128ff.

author and institution

78 Hal Foster, *Recodings*, Seattle, Wash., 1985, p. 100.

79 Cedric Price, 'Survey', *Tema Celeste*, 90, March/April 2002.

79 Maria Lind, 'Learning From Art and Artists', in Gavin Wade (ed.), *Curating in the 21st Century*, Walsall, 2000, p. 88.

79 Hans Ulrich Obrist in *The Producers: Contemporary Curators in Conversation (2)*, BALTIC, Gateshead, 2001, p. 34.

80 Brian O'Doherty, *The Gallery as Gesture*, 1981. Quoted in Yves Aupetitallot (ed.), *Wide White Space*, exh. cat., Palais des Beaux-Arts de Bruxelles, Düsseldorf, 1995, p. 7.

80 *Ibid.*

80 Ilya Kabakov, *On the 'Total Installation'*, Ostfildern, 1995, p. 271.

80 André Malraux, *Museum Without Walls*, London, 1967, p. 12.

81 Vilém Flusser, *Vom Subject zum Projekt: Menschwerdung, Schriften 3*, Düsseldorf, 1994.

81 Kasper König, 'Survey', *Tema Celeste*, 90, March/April 2002.

81 Jerôme Sans, 'Survey', *Tema Celeste*, 90, March/April 2002.

81 Àgnes Ivacs, *Locus Solus*, Book Review, Artpool Library, 2002.

81 Miwon Kwon, *One Place after Another*, Cambridge, Mass., 2002, p. 51.

exchange and interaction

106 Alicia Framis, *Blue Dogma*, exh. cat., Berlin Biennale, 2001, p. 87.

106 Nicolas Bourriaud quoted in Jemima Montagu, 'Site de création contemporaine', exhibition review, *Frieze*, 67, May 2002.

106 Paolo Bianchi, *LKW Lebenskunstwerke*, exh. cat., Kunsthaus/Kunstverein Bregenz, 2000.

106 *Ibid.*

106 Rirkrit Tiravanija and Franz Ackermann, *LKW Lebenskunstwerke*, exh. cat., Kunsthaus/Kunstverein Bregenz, 2000, p. 112.

107 Miwon Kwon, *One Place after Another*, Cambridge, Mass., 2002, p. 46.

108 Kwon, *op. cit.*, p. 50.
108 Marshall McLuhan, *Understanding Media*, London, 1964, p. 264.
109 Nicolas Bourriaud, 'Berlin Letter About Relational Aesthetics', *2. Berlin Biennale*, exh. cat., Berlin, 2001, p. 40.
109 Hou Hanru, 'On the Mid-Ground', *Timezone 8*, Hong Kong, 2002, p. 15.

time and narrative

132 Marcel Duchamp quoted in Pierre Cabanne, *Dialogues with Marcel Duchamp*, New York, 1987, p. 106.
132 Geoffrey Batchen, 'The Art of Archiving', Ingrid Schaffner and Matthias Winzen (eds), *Deep*

Storage – Collecting, Storing, and Archiving in Art, Munich and New York, 1998, p. 47.
133 Vilém Flusser, *Dinge und Undinge: Phänomelologische Skizzen*, Munich, 1993.
134 Peter Osborne, *Travelling Light*, Manchester, 2000.
134 Irit Rogoff (Beatrice von Bismark et al., eds), *Interarchive*, Cologne, 2001, p. 177.
134 Rogoff, *op.cit.*, p. 179.
134 Jane and Louise Wilson, Interview with Lisa Corrin, Serpentine Gallery, London, 1999, p. 9.
134 Paul Virilio, *Lost Dimension, Semiotext(e)*, New York, 1991.
135 Jean-François Lyotard, *The Postmodern Condition: A Report on Knowledge*, Manchester, 1984, p. 81.

the body of the audience

166 Jonathan Crary, *Suspensions of Perception: Attention, Spectacle, and Modern Culture*, Cambridge, Mass., and London, 1999, p. 1.
167 Crary, *op. cit.*, p. 74.
167 Jacques Lacan, *The Four Fundamental Concepts of Psycho-Analysis*, tr. Alan Sheridan, London, 1977, p. 80.
168 M. Christine Boyer, *The City of Collective Memory*, Cambridge, Mass., 1994.
168 Jean Baudrillard, 'The Ecstacy of Communication', *Postmodern Culture*, London, 1985, p. 128.

bibliography

Monographs and Exhibition Catalogues

Absalon, exh. cat., Tel Aviv Museum of Art, 1992
Absalon. Retrospective, exh. cat., CAPC Bordeaux, 1998
Ackermann, Franz and Rikrit Tiravanija, *RE public*, Grazer Kunstverein, Graz, 1998
Aernout Mik, exh. cat., Van AbbeMuseum, Eindhoven, 1999
Aernout Mik, Primal Gestures, Minor Roles, exh. cat., The Stedelijk Van Abbemuseum, Eindhoven, Rotterdam, 2000
Ahtila, Eija-Liisa, *Fantasized Persons and Taped Conversations*, exh. cat., Tate Modern, London, 2002
Aitken, Doug, *Diamond Sea*, London, 2000
Doug Aitken, London, 2001
Daren Almond, exh. cat., Kunsthaus Zürich, 2001
Francis Alÿs, exh. cat., Musée Picasso, Antibes, 2001
Alÿs, Francis, *The Last Clown*, exh. cat., Fundació 'La Caixa', Barcelona, 2000
Amorales, Carlos, *Los Amorales*, exh. cat., Migros Museum Zurich, Amsterdam, 2001
Ana Miguel, exh. cat., Contemporary Art Center Venâncio-Ecco, Brasília, 2001
Andrea Zittel, exh. cat., Deichtorhallen, Hamburg, 1999
Anish Kapoor/Germano Celant, London, 1996
Åsdam, Knut, *Works 1995–2000*, exh. cat., Tate Britain, Copenhagen, 2000
Atelier van Lieshout, A Manual, exh. cat., Kölnischer Kunstverein, Cologne, Museum

Boijmans Van Beuningen, Rotterdam, 1997
Atelier van Lieshout, *The Good, The Bad + The Ugly*, Rotterdam, 1998
Per Barclay, exh. cat., Galleria Civica di Arte Contemporanea, Trento, Turin, 2000
Per Barclay, exh. cat., The National Museum of Contemporary Art, Oslo, 1999
Barney, Matthew, *The Cremaster Cycle*, New York, 2002
Tatsurou Bashi alias Tazro Niscino: Obdach, exh. cat., Räume von Junge Kunst, Wolfsburg, 1997
Beecroft, Vanessa, *VB 08-36 Performances*, Ostfildern-Ruit, 2000
Bik, Liesbeth and Jos van der Pol, *Moderna Museet Project*, exh. cat., Moderna Museet Stockholm, 2001
Bill Viola, exh. cat., Whitney Museum of American Art, New York, 1999
Bill Viola, Going Forth By Day: Process/Prozess, Deutsche Guggenheim Berlin, 2002
Bock, John, *Gribbohm*, Ostfildern, 2001
Bodys Isek Kingelez, Ostfildern-Ruit, 2001
Christian Boltanski, exh. cat., Galleria d'arte moderna, Milan, 1997
Boltanski, Christian, *La vie impossible. Ce dont ils se souviennent/Woran sie sich erinnern/What People Remember About Him*, Cologne, 2001
Bonde, Peter and Jason Rhoades, *The Snowball*, Ostfildern-Ruit, 1999
Bonvicini, Monica, *Eternmale*, exh. cat., Kunsthaus Glarus and Centre d'édition contemporaine, Geneva, 2001
—, *Scream & Shake*, exh. cat., Le Magasin, Grenoble, 2001

Brüggemann, Stefan, *Intellectual Disaster*, New Mexico City, 2002
Christoph Büchel, exh. cat., Kunsthalle St Gallen, 1999
Bul, Lee, *Korean Pavilion*, exh. cat., 48th Venice Biennale, 1999.
Bulloch, Angela, *Rule Book*, London, 2001
Bunn, David, *Double Monster*, exh. cat., New York, 2000
Cardiff, Janet, *The Missing Voice (Case Study B)*, London, 2000
Christo, *The Reichstag and Urban Projects*, Munich and New York, 1993
Creed, Martin, *Works*, exh. cat., Southampton City Art Gallery, Southampton, 2000
Dalziel+Scullion, *Home*, exh. cat., Fruitmarket Gallery, Edinburgh, 2002
Dávila, Jose, *Temporality Is a Question of Survival*, exh. cat., Camden Arts Centre, London, 2001
Tacita Dean, exh. cat., Museum für Gegenwartskunst, Basle, 2001
Tacita Dean, exh. cat., Tate Britain, London, 2001
Delvoye, Wim, *New & Improved*, exh. cat., New Museum for Contemporary Art, 2002
—, *Skatalog*, exh. cat., Museumkunstpalast, Düsseldorf, 2001
Dion, Mark, *Archaeology*, London, 1999
Stan Douglas, London, 1998
Douglas, Stan, *Joumey into Fear 2001*, exh. cat., Serpentine Gallery London and Cologne, 2002
Dutton & Peacock, *On Vanishing*, exh. cat., Site Gallery, Sheffield, 2001
Olafur Eliasson, London, 2002
Eliasson, Olafur, *The Mediated Motion*,

Cologne, 2001
—, *Your only real thing is time*, exh. cat., Institute of Contemporary Art, Boston, Mass., 2001
Elmgreen, Michael & Ingar Dragset, *Taking Place*, exh. cat., Kunsthalle Zürich and Witte de With, Center for Contemporary Art, Rotterdam, 2001
Emin, Tracey, *Diary*, exh. cat., Cornerhouse, Manchester, 2000
—, *Holiday Inn*, exh. cat., Gesellschaft für Aktuelle Kunst, Bremen, 1998
Fischer, Lili, *Leporello-Arie*, Ostfildern-Ruit, 1997
Sylvie Fleury, exh. cat., Galerie der Stadt Esslingen, Villa Merkel, Ostfildern-Ruit, 1999
François, Michel, *La plante en nous/Die Pflanze in uns*, exh. cat., Kunsthalle Bern, Göttingen, 2000
Friis-Hansen, Dana, Octavia Zaya et al. (contributors), *Cai Guo-Qiang* London, 2002
Gilchrist, Bruce and Jo Joelson, *Syzygy/Polaria*, London Fieldworks, 2002
Gordon, Douglas, *Feature Film*, London, 1999
Rodney Graham, Whitechapel Art Gallery, London, 2002
Graham, Rodney, *Cinema Music Video*, exh. cat., Kunsthalle Vienna, 1999
Rodney Graham, Works from 1976 to 1994, Art Gallery of York University, Toronto, 1994
Gygi, Fabrice, *Le Magasin*, exh. cat., Centre national d'art contemporain, Grenoble, 2000
Håkanson, Henrik, *Syndrome*, exh. cat., IAPSIS, Stockholm, 2000
—, *Tomorrow and Tonight*, exh. cat., Kunsthalle Basel, 1999
Halmans, Frank, *Noodvelichting*, Hermen Molendijk Stichting, Centrum Beeldende Kunst, Amersfort, 1999
Hamilton, Ann, *Mattering*, exh. cat., Musée d'art contemporain de Montréal, 1999
—, *Myein*, exh. cat,. The United States Pavilion, 48th Venice Biennale, 1999
—, *Present-Past, 1984–1997*, exh. cat., Musée d'art contemporain de Lyon, 1998
Christine Hill, exh. cat., Galerie EIGEN+ART Berlin and Kunst-Werken, Berlin, 1995
Hill, Gary, *Projective Installations. Nr. 3*, New York, 1997
Hirschhorn, Thomas, *Jumbo Spoons and Big Cake*, exh. cat., The Art Institute of Chicago, 2000
—, *Material. Public Works -The Bridge 2000*, London, 2001
Hirst, Damien, *I want to spend the rest of my life everywhere, with everyone, one to one, always, forever, now*, London, 1997
—, *Theories, Models, Methods, Approaches, Assumptions, Results and Findings*, Gagosian Gallery, New York, 2000
Höller, Carsten, *Glück/Skop*, exh. cat., Kunstverein Hamburg, 1996
—, *Registro*, exh. cat. Fondazione Prada, Milan, 2000

Höller, Carsten and Rosemarie Trockel, *Ein Haus für Schweine und Menschen*, Cologne, 1997
Hoptman, Laura J., *Yayoi Kusama*, London, 2000
Huyghe, Pierre, *The Third Memory*, Editions du Centre Pompidou, Paris, 2000
Christian Jankowski: Play, exh. cat., De Appel, Amsterdam, 2001
Janssens, Ann Veronica, *Une image différente dans chaque œil*, Liège and Brussells, 1999
Ilya Kabakov, Milan, 2001
Kabakov, Ilya, *Installations 1983-1995*, exh. cat., Le Musée national d'art moderne Centre de création industrielle, Paris, 1995
—, *Installations, Catalogue Raisonné 1983-2000*, Düsseldorf, 2000
—, *The Man Who Never Threw Anything Away*, New York, 1996
Kabakov, Ilya and Emilia, *Palace of Projects*, Düsseldorf, 1998
Katase, Kazuo, *Umsicht*, exh. cat., Wilhelm-Hack-Museum, Ludwigshafen am Rhein, Cologne, 1999
Tadashi Kawamata, exh. cat., Middelheimmuseum Antwerpen, 2000
Kruger, Barbara, *Remote Control*, Cambridge, Mass., London, 1993
Kuball, Mischa, *Private Light/Public Light*, exh. cat., 24. Biennale São Paulo, Ostfildern-Ruit, 1998
—, *Project Rooms*, Cologne, 1997
Landy, Michael, *Break Down*, exh. cat., London, 2002
Lane, Abigail, *Tomorrows World, Yesterday Fever (Mental Guests Incorporated)*, exh. cat., Milton Keynes Gallery, London, 2001
Leal, Miguel, *Projecto Bunker (1996-99)*, exh. cat., Circulo de Artes Plásticas de Coimbra, 2000
Maurizio Cattelan, London, 2000
Mori, Mariko, *Dream Temple*, exh. cat., Fondation Prada, Milan, 1999
—, *Esoteric Cosmos*, exh. cat., Kunstmuseum Wolfsburg, 1999
Muñoz, Juan, *Double Bind*, exh. cat, Tate Modern, London, 2001
Muntean/Rosenblum, *Where else*, Secession, Vienna, 2000
Nelson, Mike, *A Fotgotten Kingdom*, London, 2001
Newling, John, *Weight*, exh. cat. Turnpike Gallery, Leigh, 1998
Nicolai, Olaf, *...fading in, fading out, fading away...*, exh. cat., Westfälischer Kunstverein, Münster, 2001
—, *Show Case*, Nuremberg, 1999
Op de Beeck, Hans, *A Selection of Works 1996-2001*, Amsterdam 2001
Julian Opie, exh. cat., Ikon Gallery, Birmingham, 2001
Otto, Catrin, *Einschnitte*, exh. cat., Goldrausch 11, Berlin, 2000
João Penalva, exh. cat., Frac Languedoc-Roussillon and Camden Arts Centre, 1999

Petry, Michael, *The Trouble with Michael*, London, 2001
Pilis, Alexander, *Architecture Parallax: SnackLunch*, exh. cat., St Norbert Arts and Cultural Center, Winnipeg, 1996
Pippin, Steven, *Addendum*, exh. cat., Portikus, Frankfurt am Main, 1994
Jaume Plensa: Love Songs, exh. cat., Kestner Gesellschaft, Hanover, 1999
Rawanchaikul, Navin, *Comm...: Individual and Collaborative Projects 1993-1999*, Cologne, 1999
Rehberger, Tobias, *(whenever you need me)*, exh. cat., Westfälischer Kunstverein, Münster, 2001
—, *Apples and Pears*, Cologne, 2002
Rist, Pipilotti, *Apricots Along The Street*, exh. cat., Museo Reina Sofia, Madrid, Zurich, 2001
Pipilotti Rist, London, 2001
Rondinone, Ugo, *Guided by Voices*, exh. cat., Kunsthaus Glarus and Ostfildern-Ruit, 1999
—, *Hell, Yes!*, Küsnacht, 2000
Sæthre, Børre, *A Million Dreams – A Million Scars*, exh. cat., Galleri Wang, Oslo, 1999
Gregor Schneider, exh. cat., Musée d'Art Moderne de la Ville de Paris, 1998
Schneider, Gregor, *Totes Haus Ur*, Ostfildern-Ruit, 2001
Roman Signer, exh. cat., Swiss Pavilion, 1999
Venice Biennale, St Gallen, 1999
Smith, Terry, *Site Unseen*, London 1997
Sudell, Louise, *Theatre of Ideas*, exh. cat., Picaron Editions, Amsterdam, 1990
Do-Ho Suh, exh. cat., Whitney Museum of American Art, New York, 2001
Sam Taylor-Wood, exh. cat. Hayward Gallery, London, 2002
Taylor-Wood, Sam, *Third Party*, Ostfildern-Ruit, 2000
Diana Thater, Delphine, Secession, Vienna, 2000
Tiravanija, Rikrit, *Untitled*, exh. cat., Migros Museum für Gegenwartskunst, Zurich, 1998
Tolaas, Sissel, *Transitionen*, Ostfildern-Ruit, 1994
Torres, Francesc, *The Repository of Absent Flesh*, exh. cat., List Visual Arts Center, Cambridge, Mass., 1998
Tuerlinckx, Joëlle, *Autour de Film. Cinema. Audio and Visual Days. Journal de Jours. Expositions. Projections*, exh. cat., Brussels, 2000
Tunick, Spencer, *Self*, DeBeyerd Centrum voor Beeldende Kunst, Breda, 2001
Tyson, Keith, *Supercollider*, exh. cat., South London Gallery, 2002
Weigand, Hans, *Jerry Cotto 2002*, Cologne, 2002
Westphalen, Olav, *E.S.U.S. & other works*, exh. cat., Public Art Fund, New York, 2002
Wexler, Allan, *The Fine Art of Applied Art*, Nuremberg, 1997
Wilson, Jane and Louise, *Ellipsis*, London, 2001

Reference Books

Installation

Arscott, Caroline (ed.), *On installation*, vol. 24 (no. 2), Oxford, 2002

Bahtsetzis, Sotirios, *Der Anfang der Installationskunst*, Berlin, 2003

Kabakov, Ilya and Boris Groys, *Die Kunst der Installation*, Munich, 1996

Kachur, Lewis, *Displaying the Marvelous. Marcel Duchamp, Salvador Dali and Surrealist Exhibition Installations*, Cambridge, Mass., and London, 2001

Kaye, Nick, *Site-specific Art. Performance, Place and Documentation*, London and New York, 2000

de Oliveira, Nicolas, Nicola Oxley and Michael Petry, *Installation Art*, London and Washington, D.C., 1994

Reiss, Julie H., *From Margin to Center. The Spaces of Installation Art*, Cambridge, Mass., and London, 2000

Suderburg, Erika (ed.), *Space, Site, Intervention. Situating Installation Art*, Minneapolis, Minn., and London, 2000

Display

Andriesse, Paul (ed.), *Art Gallery Exhibiting. The Gallery as a Vehicle of Art*, Eindhoven, 1996

Barker, Ema (ed.), *Contemporary Cultures of Display*, London, 1999

Bovier, Lionel and Christophe Cherix (ed.), *Independent Spaces*, Geneva, 1999

Greenberg, Reesa, Bruce W. Ferguson and Sandy Nairne (ed.), *Thinking about Exhibitions*, London and New York, 1996

Putnam, James, *Art and Artifact. The Museum as Medium*, London and New York, 2001

Staniszewski, Mary Anne, *The Power of Display. A History of Exhibition Installations at the Museum of Modern Art*, Cambridge, Mass., and London, 1998

Archive

Bismarck, Beatrice von, et al., *Interarchive*, Cologne, 2002

Clifford, James, *On Collecting Art and Culture*, Cambridge, Mass., 1995

Elsner, John and Roger Cardinal, *Cultures of Collecting*, London, 1994

Groy, Boris, *Die Logik der Sammlung*, Munich, 1997

Site specificity

Büttner, Claudia, *Art Goes Public. Von der Gruppenausstellung im Freien zum Projekt im nicht-institutionellen Raum*, Munich, 1997

Crimp, Douglas, *On the Museum's Ruins*, Cambridge, Mass., and London, 1993

Kwon, Miwon, *One Place after Another. Site-Specific Art and Locational Identity*, Cambridge, Mass., and London, 2001

Möntmann, Nina, *Kunst als sozialer Raum*, Cologne, 2002

Site and Displacement

Augé, Marc, *Non-places: Introduction to an Anthropology of Supermodernity*, London and New York, 1995

Bell, Michael and Sze Tsung Leong (ed.), *Slow Space*, New York, 1998

Borden, Iain, Jane Rendell et al., *The Unknown City*, Cambridge, Mass., and London, 2000

Burgin, Victor, *In/different Spaces: Place and Memory in Visual Culture*, Berkeley and Los Angeles, Calif., and London, 1996

Clarke, David B. (ed.), *The Cinematic City*, London and New York, 1997

Crang, Mike and Nigel Thrift (eds), *Thinking Space*, London and New York, 2000

Deutsche, Rosalyn, *Art and Spatial Politics*, Cambridge, Mass., and London, 1996

Grosz, Elisabeth A., *Architecture from the Outside: Essays on Virtual and Real Space*, Cambridge, Mass., and London, 2001

Kaplan, Caren, *Questions of Travel: Postmodern Discourses of Displacement*, Durham, N.C., 1996

Lacy, Suzanne, *Mapping the Terrain. New Genre Public Art*, Seattle, Wash., 1995

Lippard, Lucy R., *On the Beaten Track: Tourism, Art and Place*, New York, 2000

Low, Seth M., *On the Plaza: The Politics of Public Space and Culture*, Austin, Tex., 2000

Mathews, Gordon, *Global Culture/Individual Identity*, London and New York, 2000

McKenzie, Evan, *Privatopia*, New Haven, Conn., 1994

Morley, David and Keith Robins, *Spaces of Identity*, London and New York, 1995

Osborne, Peter D., *Traveling light: Photography, Travel and Visual Culture*, Manchester and New York, 2000

Vidler, Anthony, *Warped Space. Art, Architecture, and Anxiety in Modern Culture*, Cambridge, Mass., London, 2000

Weibel, Peter (ed.), *Olafur Eliasson: Surroundings Surrounded. Essays on Space and Science*, Cambridge, Mass., and London, 2000

Art in Context

Bätschmann, Oskar, *The Artist in the Modern World: The Conflict Between Market and Self-Expression*, Cologne, 1997

Jones, Caroline A., *Machine In The Studio: Constructing The Postwar American Artist*, Chicago, Ill., 1996

Weibel, Peter (ed.), *Kontext Kunst*, Cologne, 1994

Wu, Chin-Tao, *Privatising Culture. Corporate Art Intervention Since the 1980s*, London, 2002

Perception and Representation

Crary, Jonathan, *Suspensions of Perception: Attention, Spectacle, and Modern Culture*, Cambridge, Mass., and London, 1999

Foster, Hal, The Return of the Real: *The Avant-garde at the End of the Century*, Cambridge, Mass., and London, 1996

Krauss, Rosalind, *A Voyage on the North Sea: Art in the Age of Post-Medium Condition*, London, 1999, and New York, 2000

Manovich, Lev, T*he Language of New Media*, Cambridge, Mass., and London, 2001

McEvilley, Thomas, *Sculpture in the Age of Doubt*, New York, 1999

Rieser, Martin and Andrea Zapp, *New Screen Media: Cinema/Art/Narrative*, London, 2002

Body as Site

Jappe, Elisabeth, *Performance, Ritual. Prozess – Handbuch der Aktionskunst in Europa*, Munich and New York, 1993

Jones, Amelia, *Body Art: Performing The Subject*, Minneapolis, Minn., 1998

Sandford, Mariellen R. (ed.), *Happenings and Other Acts*, London and New York, 1995

Schimmel, Paul (ed.), *Out of Actions: Between Performance and the Object, 1949–1979*, London, 1998

Virtual Environment and Simulation

Hayles, N. Katherine, *How We Became Posthuman: Virtual Bodies in Cybernetics and Literature*, Chicago, Ill., 1999

Holtzman, Steven R., *Digital Mosaics: the Aesthetics of Cyberspace*, New York, 1997

Mitchell, William J., *City of Bits: Space, Place, and the Infobahn*, Cambridge, Mass., and London, 1996

Moser, Mary Anne with Douglas MacLeod (ed.), *Immersed in Technology. Art and Virtual Environments*, Cambridge, Mass., and London, 1996

Negroponte, Nicholas, *Being Digital*, London and New York, 1995

Virilio, Paul, *A Landscape of Events*, Cambridge, Mass., and London, 2000

Weibel, Peter and Timothy Druckrey (ed.), *Net Condition: Art and Global Media*, Cambridge, Mass., Karlsruhe and London, 2001

Wilson, Stephen, *Information Arts. Intersections of Art, Science, and Technology*, Cambridge, Mass., and London, 2001

Memory and fictional topographies

Amato, Joseph Anthony, Dust: *A History of the Small and the Invisible*, Berkeley and Los Angelesl, Calif., and London, 2000

Batchelor, David, *Chromophobia*, London, 2000

Bibliomania, exh. cat., The Henry Moore Foundation, London, 1999

Calvino, Italo, *Invisible Cities*, London, 1997
(originally published in 1972 as *Le Città invisibili*)
Coles, Alex (ed.), *The Optic of Walter Benjamin*,
London, 1999
Derrida, Jacques, *Archive Fever: A Freudian
Impression*, London, 1996
Harbison, Robert, *Eccentric Spaces*, Cambridge,
Mass., London, 2000
Manguel, Alberto and Gianni Guadalupi (ed.), *The
Dictionary of Imaginary Places*, London, 1999
Olalquiaga, Celeste, *The Artificial Kingdom. A
Treasury of the Kitsch Expirience*, London, 1998
Perec, George, *Species of Space and Other Pieces*,
London and New York, 1997
Robbe-Grillet, Alain, *Topography of a Phantom City*,
London, 1978
Stewart, Susan, *On Longing. Narratives of the
Miniature, the Gigantic, the Souvenir, the Collection*,
Durham, N.C., and London, 1993

Mass Culture

Buck-Morss, Susan, *Dreamworld and Catastrophe.
The Passing of Mass Utopia in East and West*,
Cambridge, Mass., and London, 2000
Chaney, Davis, *Lifestyles*, London and
New York, 1996
Frisa, Maria Luisa, Mario Lupano and Stefano
Tonchi, *Total Living*, Milan, 2002
Lehmann, Ulrich, *Tigersprung. Fashion in
Modernity*, Cambridge, Mass., and London, 2000
Miller, Daniel, *A Theory of Shopping*, Ithaca,
New York, 1998
Tester, Keith (ed.), *The Flâneur*, London and New
York, 1994

Statements

Detterer, Gabriele (ed.), *Art Recollection. Artists,
Interviews and Statements in the Nineties*, Ravenna,
1997
Finkelpearl, Tom (ed.), *Dialogues on Public Art*,
Cambridge, Mass., and London, 2000
Hiller, Susan and Sarah Martin (ed.),
*The Producers: Contemporary Curators in
Conversation*, Gateshead 2000 and Newcastle upon
Tyne, 2001
Ramos, María Elena (ed.), *Intervenciones
en el espacio. Diálogos en el MBA*,
Caracas, 1998
Sâns, Jérome and Marc Sanchez (ed.),
TokyoBook1, 'What do you expect from an art
institution in the 21th century?', Paris, 2001
Wade, Gavin (ed.), *Curating in 21st Century*,
Walsall, 2000

list of illustrations

Courtesy: the artist and Elba Benítez Gallery, Madrid (collection of the Bohen Foundation, New York).

p. 44 (above right) Francesc Torres
The Crystal Continent (El continent de cristall), 1993–94
Mixed media, 60 x 20 m (197 x 66 ft) Site: Tinglado 2, Tarragona, Spain. Photo Martín García, Barcelona. Courtesy: the artist and Elba Benítez Gallery, Madrid.

p. 45 Steven Pippin
Born 1960 in UK.
Addendum, 1994.
Photonegative on cardboard, 4.6 x 7.6 m (15 ft x 24 ft 11 in.). Installation view: Portikus Frankfurt am Main, Germany, 1994–95. Courtesy: Klosterfelde, Berlin.

p. 46 staatsbankberlin
Einstein On The Beach, 2002
View of the main hall. Opera in four acts by Philip Glass and Robert Wilson
opera/installation idea, concept and stage director: Berthold Schneider; musical director: Ari Benjamin Meyers; installation concept: Veronika Witte; choreography: Tino Sehgal; costumes: Nina Thorwart; singers and staatsbankberlin orchestra. Courtesy: staatsbankberlin.

p. 47 Monica Bonvicini
1965 Born in Italy (Venice); lives and works in Berlin and Los Angeles.
Plastered, 1998
Drywall panels, styrofoam, adaptable dimensions. Courtesy: Chouakri Brahms Berlin.

escape

p. 53 Biefer/Zgraggen
Marcel Biefer, born 1959; lives and works in Düsseldorf and Zurich.
Beat Zgraggen, born 1958.
God, 1998
Styrofoam, construction foam, electronically controlled illumination. 8.4 m (27 ft 6 in.) diameter. Installation view: Neustadtbahnhof, Bremen, Germany. Courtesy: the artists (Biefer/Zgraggen) and Horst Griese.

p. 54 (above) Per Barclay
Born 1955 in Norway.
Pas de deux, 2001
Room constructed from wooden panels, metal gantry, 2 chainsaws, 5 x 7 x 3.05 m (16 ft 5 in. x 23 ft x 10 ft). Installation view Bergen Kunstforening, Bergen, Norway. Photograph: Fin Serck Hansen, Oslo. Courtesy: Galleri Wang, Oslo.

p. 54 (below) Per Barclay
Untitled, 1999–2000
Installations 1991–2000. Installation view, exhibition at the Museum of Installation, 2000. Photograph: David Grandorge. Courtesy: the Museum of Installation, London, and Galleria Persano, Italy.

p. 55 Lee Bul
Born in 1964 in South Korea (Seoul); lives and works in Seoul.
Gravity Greater Than Velocity ll, 1999
Polycarbonate panels, steel frame, velour, sponge, karaoke equipment, LCD monitor, 250 x 184 x 120 cm (8 ft 2 in. x 6 ft x 3 ft 11 in.). Photograph: Rhee Jae-yong. Courtesy: PKM Gallery, Inc., Seoul, Korea.

p. 56 + 57 (above) Ann Veronica Janssens
Born 1956 in UK
Blue, Red and Yellow, 2001
Installation at the Neuenationale Galerie, Berlin. Photograph: the artist. Courtesy: the artist.

p. 56 + 57 (below) Bruce Gilchrist and Jo Joelson
Both Born in UK
Polaria, 2002
3 m cube. Installation view: Wapping Hydraulic Power Station, London. Photograph: Lenard Smith, Anthony Oliver, Stephen Morgan. Courtesy: London Fieldworks.

p. 58 Jaume Plensa
Born 1955 in Spain
Love Sounds I–V, 1998
Alabaster, iron, plastic, light and sound
212 x 120 x 228 cm/212 x 120 x 115 cm (7 ft x 4 ft x 7 ft 6 in./7 ft x 4 ft x 3 ft 10 in.). Installation view: the Kestner Gesellschaft, Hannover, Germany, 1999. Photograph: Gunter Lepkowski. Courtesy: the artist and Galeria Toni Tàpies, Barcelona.

p. 59 (left + below) Ernesto Neto
Born 1964 in Brazil; lives and works in Rio de Janeiro.
Walking in Venus blue cave, 2001
Stocking, styrofoam, buttons, incandescent lights, 396.2 x 777.2 x 833 cm (13 ft x 25 ft 6 in. x 27 ft 4 in.). Courtesy: the artist and Tanya Bonakdar Gallery, New York (collection Kent and Vicki Logan, Vail, Co.).

p. 59 (above right) Pipilotti Rist
Born 1962 in Switzerland.
Sip My Ocean (Grossmut Begatte Mich), 1994–96
Video, dimensions variable. Courtesy: the artist and Luhring Augustine Gallery, New York.

p. 60 (right) Siobhan Hapaska
Born in 1963 in Northen Ireland (Belfast); lives and works in London.
Here, 1995
Fibreglass, opalescent paint, acrylic lacquer, lambswool, harness, piped water and oxygen, 100.3 x 400 x 200 cm (3 ft 4 in. x 13 ft 1 in. x 6 ft 6 in.). Courtesy: Tanya Bonakdar Gallery, New York.

p. 60 (left) Absalon
Born 1964 in Israel (Ashold); died in Paris 1993.
Cellule nr. 6, 1992
Wood, cardboard, white paint, 300 x 220 x 220 cm (9 ft 10 in. x 7 ft 2 in. x 7 ft 2 in.). Photograph: Ann Katrin Blomqvist. Collection Magasin 3 Stockholm Konsthall. Courtesy: Magasin 3 Stockholm Konsthall.

p. 61 Børre Sæthre
Born 1967 in Norway.
MY PRIVATE SKY, unit 1/trauma white, 2001
Installation view: Astrup Fearnley Museum of Modern Art, Oslo, 2001. Photograph: the artist. Courtesy: Galleri Wang, Oslo.

p. 61 (right) Gregor Schneider
Born 1969 in Germany.
ur12, total isoliertes Gästezimmer, Rheydt, 1995
Courtesy: the artist, VG Bildkunst, Bonn and Galerie Luis Campaña, Cologne.

p. 62 Mischa Kuball
Born 1959 in Germany.
Believe/Disbelieve, 1999
Installation view of the exhibition 'Project Rooms', the Museum of Installation, London. Photograph: Edward Woodman. Courtesy: the artist and the Museum of Installation, London.

p. 63 Kazuo Katase
Born 1947 in Japan.
Winterreise, 1998
White house: wood, gypsum, floor: white felt, 1 swing, see-saw: white wax, blue filtered light. Installation view Overbeck-Gesellschaft, Lübeck, Germany. Photograph: the artist. Courtesy: the artist.

p. 64 (above) Pierre Huyghe
Born 1962 in France (Paris). Lives and works in Paris.
L'expédition scintillante, a musical, Act 1, Act 2, Act 3, 2002
Exhibition view Kunsthaus Bregenz. Photograph: KuB, Markus Tretter. Courtesy: Marian Goodman Gallery, New York/Paris.

p. 64 (below) Yayoi Kusama
Born 1929 Matsumoto-shi Naganoken, Japan.
Dots Obsession, 2000
Dimensions variable. Photograph: André Morin. Courtesy: Le Consortium, Dijon, France.

p. 65 Jon Lockhart and Tom Cox-Bisham
Jon Thomas: Together in Electric Dreams, 2002
Installation view: the Museum of Installation, London, mixed media. Photograph: David Grandorge. Courtesy: the artists and the Museum of Installation, London.

p. 66 Julian Opie
Born 1958 in UK (London).
Imagine that you are moving (detail), 1997
Lightbox and computer installation. Photograph: Stephen White. Courtesy: the artist and the Lisson Gallery, London.

p. 67 Ugo Rondinone
Born 1963 in Switzerland.
It's late and the wind carries a faint sound as it moves..., 1999–2000
6 video projections, 12 video loops, sound, dimensions variable. Installation view 'GUIDED BY VOICES' exhibition, Kunsthaus Glarus, Switzerland, 1999. Courtesy: Matthew Marks Gallery, New York.

author and institution

Hales Gallery, London.

p. 88 (above) Mark Dion
Born 1961 in USA (New Bedford, Massachusetts); lives and works in Beach Lake, Pennsylvania.
Alexander Wilson Studio, 1999
Wooden structure, mixed media, dimensions variable. Courtesy: the artist and Tanya Bonakdar Gallery, New York.

p. 88 (below) Jorge Pardo
Born 1963 in Cuba (Havana); lives and works in Los Angeles (California).
Pier, 1997
Redwood, metal, cigarette vending machine. Installation view Skulptur Project Münster 1997. Courtesy: the artist and Friedrich Petzel Gallery, New York.

p. 89 Ayşe Erkmen
Born 1949 in Turkey; lives in Berlin and Istanbul.
Sculptures on Air, 1997
1 helicopter, 13 sculptures, museum. Exhibiting site: Münster/Westfälisches Landesmuseum. Photograph: the artist. Courtesy: the artist and Sculpture Projects Münster, 1997.

p. 90 (below) Hans Haacke
Born 1936 in Germany (Cologne); lives and works in New York.
Der Bevölkerung (To the Population), 1999–2000
Installation site: Reichstag, Berlin
Oblong wooden trough, 6.8 x 20.8 x 1.2 m (22 ft 4 in. x 66 ft 6 in. x 4 ft), 14 white neon letters, 1.2 m (3 ft 11 in.) high, soil, unencumbered plant growth
Courtesy: the artist. Credit: VG Bild-Kunst.

p. 90 + 91 Christo and Jeanne-Claude
Both born 1935.
Wrapped Reichstag, Berlin, 1971–1995
Photograph: Wolfgang Volz. Courtesy: Christo and Jeanne-Claude.

p. 92 Anish Kapoor
Born 1954 in India (Bombay); lives and works in London.
Tarantara, 1999
PVC. Installation view: BALTIC, Newcastle, England. Photograph: Ravi Deepres. Courtesy: Barbara Gladstone Gallery, New York.

p. 93 (right) Daniel Pflumm
Born 1968 in Switzerland (Geneva); lives and works in Berlin.
Ohne Titel, 1998
Lightbox on the façade of the South London Gallery. Photograph: John Mason. Courtesy: Galerie Neu, Berlin & South London Gallery, London.

p. 93 (above) Thomas Hirschhorn
Born 1957 in Switzerland (Berne). Lives and works in Paris.
World Airport/Flugplatz Welt, 1999
Mixed media, 500 m² (5382 ft²). Exhibition view at the Venice Biennale. Courtesy: the artist and Galerie Chantal Crousel.

p. 93 (below) Micah Lexier
Born 1960 in Canada.
Ampersand: A Project for the Sheppard/Leslie Subway Station, Toronto (open in 2002).
17,000 custom-printed ceramic tiles 77.4 cm² (12 in.²). Commissioned by the Toronto Transit Commission. Courtesy: the artist and Toronto Transit Commission.

p. 94 Barbara Bloom
Born 1951 in USA.
Pictures from the Floating World, 1995
Installation view: Leo Castelli Gallery, New York. Mixed media. Courtesy: Gorney Bravin+Lee, New York.

p. 95 Tatsurou Bashi (alias Tazro Niscino)
Born 1960 in Japan (Nagoya).
Villa Victoria, 2002
Installation at Derby Square, Liverpool, Sept.–Nov.2002. Mixed media, dimensions variable. Courtesy: the artist.

p. 96 (above) Stefan Brüggemann
Capitalism and Schizophrenia, 2003
Puerto Rico. Dimensions variable. Courtesy: the artist.

p. 96 (below) Micah Lexier
The Hall of Names, 1996
Laser-cut stainless steel, 243.8 m (800 ft) long. Commissioned for the National Trade Centre, Toronto. Courtesy: the artist.

p. 97 (above) Elmgreen & Dragset
Michael Elmgreen born 1961 in Denmark, Ingar Dragset born 1969 in Norway.
Powerless Structures, Fig. 111, 2001
Installation view: Portikus Frankfurt am Main, Germany, 2001. Courtesy: Klosterfelde, Berlin, Nicolai Wallner, Copenhagen and Tanya Bonakdar, New York.

p. 97 (below) Elmgreen & Dragset
Taking Place, 2001–2002
Site specific project: remodelling of the exhibition space Kunsthalle Zürich. Photograph: Burkhard Meltzer. Courtesy: Kunsthalle Zürich.

p. 98 Miguel Leal
Born 1967 in Portugal (Oporto); lives and works in Oporto.
Bunker Project, 1999
CAPC, Coimbra, Portugal, 1999. Mixed media, dimensions variable. Photograph: José Meneses. Courtesy: the artist and Galeria Marta Vidal.

p. 99 Joëlle Tuerlinckx
Born 1958 in Belgium
In Real Time, Space Parts/Night Cabin/Solar-room, 2002
Installation view: the South London Gallery, London. Photograph: Marcus Leith. Courtesy: the artist and the South London Gallery.

p. 100 Michel François
Born 1956 in Belgium; lives and works in Brussels.
Bureau Augmenté, 1998

Installation, Albi, Berlin, Paris, Charleroi. Mixed media. Courtesy: carlier/gebauer.

p. 101 (above + below) Dutton/Peacock
Steve Dutton and Percy Peacock live and work in the UK.
Apocotropes, 1996-97
Prints on M.D.F. Courtesy: the artists.

p. 101 (below) Dutton/Peacock
Europe, 1999
Mail shot. Courtesy: the artists.

p. 102 John Newling
Born 1952 in UK.
Weight, 1998
Mixed media. Installation view: the Turnpike Gallery, Leigh, Greater Manchester, UK. Commissioned for Arttranspennine 98. Photograph: Paula Latham. Courtesy: the artist and the Turnpike Gallery, Leigh.

p. 103 Henrik Plenge Jakobsen
Born 1967 in Denmark.
Diary of Plasma, 1995–96
Mixed media, c. 1000 x 400 x 300 cm (328 ft x 13 ft x 9 ft 10 in.). Installation Louisiana Museum, Copenhagen, Denmark and FRAC Champagne Ardennes, France. Photograph: Bent Byberg. Courtesy: the artist and Galleri Nicolai Wallner, Copenhagen.

p. 104 (above) Martin Creed
Born 1968 in UK
Work No 270 'The Lights Off', 2001
Mixed media, dimensions variable. Photograph: Achim Kukulis. Courtesy: Johnen & Schöttle, Cologne, Germany.

p. 104 (below) Renato Niemis
[;], 1994
Installation view: the Museum of Installation, London. Photograph: Edward Woodman. Courtesy: the artist and the Museum of Installation, London.

p. 105 Hew Locke
Born in UK (Edinburgh).
Cardboard Palace, 2002
Cut cardboard and paint, variable size. Installation view: the Chisenhale Gallery, London. Photograph: Stephen White
Courtesy: the artist and Chisenhale Gallery, London.

exchange and interaction

p. 110 Cai Guo-Qiang
Born 1957 in China (Quanzhou City, Fulian Province).
Cultural Melting Bath, 1997
Hot tub with hydrotherapy jets, Chinese herbal medicine, banyan tree roots, translucent fabric, live birds, taihusu rocks, triangular space: 7.3 m h x 20.4 x 24.6 x 25.3 m (24 ft h x 67 x 81 x 83 ft). Installation view: the Queens Museum of Art, New York, USA. Photograph: Hiro Ihara. Courtesy: the artist.

time and narrative

Projection with sound U-matic and CD
c. 3.6 x 4.5 m (12 x 15 ft). Photograph: Stephen
White. Courtesy: Jay Joplin/White Cube, London.
© the artist.

p. 140 (above) David Davies
Row 01, 2001
View of the installation at the Museum of
Installation, London. Photograph: David
Grandorge. Courtesy: the artist and the Museum
of Installation, London.

p. 140 (below) Massimo Bartolini
Born 1962 in Italy (Cecina); lives and works in
Cecina, Italy.
Zwei Horizonte (particolare), 2002
Furniture, tile floor, fibreglass, light equipment,
415 x 550 x 1,500 cm (13 ft 7 in. x 18 ft x 49 ft 2 in.).
Manifesta 4. Frankensteiner Hof. Photo Bernd
Bodtlander. Courtesy: Galeria Massimo De
Carlo, Milan.

p. 141 (above) Juan Cruz
Born 1970 in Spain (Valencia); lives and works
in London.
Driving Back, 1999–2000
Sound, speakers. Installation view: the Camden
Arts Centre, London. Courtesy: Matt's Gallery,
London and Camden Arts Centre, London.

p. 141 (below) 'Archive',
Group Exhibition, 1995
View of the exhibition 'Archive': Museum of
Installation, 1995. Exhibition devised by Museum
of Installation in collaboration with architects
Simon Miller and Alain Chiaradia. Photograph:
Edward Woodman. Courtesy: Simon Miller, Alain
Chiaradia and the Museum of Installation, London.

p. 142 Jason Rhoades
Born 1965 in USA.
The Great Sea Battles of Wilhelm, 1994–95
Dimensions and materials variable. Installation
view: 'Deep Storage' exhibition at Haus der Kunst,
Munich, Germany. Courtesy: David Zwirner,
New York.

p. 143 (above) Tracey Emin
Born 1963 in UK (London); lives and works
in London.
My Bed, 1998
Mattress, linens, pillows, rope, various
memorabilia, 79 x 211 x 234 cm (31 x 83 x 92 in.).
Installation view: Tate Britain, London.
Photograph: Stephen White. Courtesy: Jay
Joplin/White Cube, London. © the artist.

p. 143 (below) Liza Lou
Born 1969 in USA (New York); lives and works in
Los Angeles.
Trailer, 1999–2000
Mixed media, 365 x 243 x 609 cm (12 x 8 x 20 ft).
Courtesy: the artist and Deitch Projects, New York.

p. 144 (above) Ann Hamilton
Born 1956 in USA.
Mattering, 1997
Room dimension: 5 x 3 x 2 m (16 ft 8 in. x 10 ft 8
in. x 6 ft), typewriter ribbon, spindle, porcelain ink

pot, five peacocks, wood and steel perches 3.2 m h
(10 ft); silk 3 x 1.5 m d (9 ft 8 in. x 5 ft d circular
cutout), motors, cables, wood utility pole, wood
and steel seat, safety belt, figure, recorded voice:
audio tape, audio tape player. Installation view of
the exhibition 'Ann Hamilton: Present-Past,
1984–1997': the Musée d'art contemporain de
Lyon, France. Photograph: Thibault Jeanson.
Courtesy: Sean Kelly Gallery, New York.

p. 144 (below) Dermot O'Brien
Lives and works in the UK.
Untitled, 1995
Installation view: the Museum of Installation,
London. Photograph: Edward Woodman. Courtesy:
the artist and the Museum of Installation, London.

p. 145 (above) Sam Taylor-Wood
Born 1967 in UK (London); lives and works
in London.
Third Party, 1999
Seven 16 mm film projections with sound
(duration: 10 min.). Courtesy: Jay Joplin/White
Cube, London. © the artist.

p. 145 (below right) David Wilkinson
Untitled, 1996
Latex, pigment, video projection, convex mirrors,
lighting gel. Courtesy: the artist and empty rooms
e.V., Berlin.

p. 145 (below left) David Wilkinson
Untitled, 1999
16mm loop, aluminium, ripstop nylon, sherman
tank, slip ring. Installation view of the exhibition
'Day for Night': the Museum of Installation,
London. Photograph: Edward Woodman. Courtesy:
the artist and the Museum of Installation, London.

p. 146 Damien Hirst
Born 1965 in UK.
Love Lost (Large River Fish), 2000
Aquatic tank and filtration unit, couch, table, stool,
surgical instruments, computer ring, cup, watch
and fish. 274.3 x 213.4 x 213.4 cm (9 ft x 7 ft x 7ft).
Courtesy: Damien Hirst/Science Ltd. and Gagosian
Gallery, New York.

p. 147 (above) Phyllida Barlow
Born 1944; lives in London.
Depot, 1995
Installation view: the Museum of Installation,
London. Photograph: Edward Woodman. Courtesy:
the artist and the Museum of Installation, London.

p. 147 (below left) Knut Åsdam
Born 1968 in Norway (Trondheim).
Psychasthenia (5), 1998
Architectural installation with video programme,
17.5 x 10.5 x 3 m (57 ft 5 in. x 34 ft 5 in. x 9 ft 10
in.). Installation in 3 sections (installation detail:
view of entrance to video-booths). Installation
view: the Pakkhus, Momentum Biennial of Nordic
Art, Norway. Photograph: Stein Jørgensen, Oslo.
Courtesy: the artist; Galeria Sonia Rosso,
Pordenone/Torino, Italy; Klemens Gasser & Tanja
Grunert Inc, New York.

p. 147 (below right) Mona Hatoum
Born 1952 in Lebanon (Beirut).
Homebound, 2000
Installation view: Tate Britain, London. Kitchen
utensils, furniture, electric wire, light bulbs,
computerised dimmer switch, amplifier, speakers,
dimensions variable. Photograph: Edward
Woodman. Courtesy: Jay Jopling/White Cube,
London. © the artist.

p. 148 (above) Hans Op de Beeck
Born 1969 in Belgium.
Border, 2001
Video installation, variable length and edit
(3 versions/languages), projection of 12 m w
x 9 m h (39 ft 4 in. w x 29 ft 6 in.), DVD video, video
projector, amplifier and speakers. View at the Big
Biennial, Torino (Italy). Photograph: Gert Op de
Beeck and Hans Op de Beeck. Courtesy:
the artist.

p. 148 (below) Alexander Brodsky
Born 1955 in Russia.
Coma, 2000–2001
Mixed media, 290 x 800 x 400 cm (9 ft 6 in. x 26 ft 3
in. x 13 ft). Installation view: the Palazzo della
Triennale, Milan, Italy. Photograph: Mario
Tedeschi, Milan. Courtesy: Municipality of Milan
and Museo del Presente, Milan.

p. 149 (above) Hans Op de Beeck
Location I, 1998
Installation view: the Museum of Installation,
London, 2002, 8 m² (86 ft²) model, 200 x 260 x 310
cm (6 ft 5 in. x 8 ft 5 in. x 10 ft), waist height, wood,
polystyrene, sand, modelling paste, PVC, plastics,
plexiglas, lets, electronics, paint, light box.
Photograph: David Grandorge. Courtesy: the artist
and the Museum of Installation, London.

p. 149 (below) Marc Quinn
Born 1964 in UK (London).
Garden, 2000
Refrigerating room, stainless steel, acrylic tank,
heated glass, refrigeration equipment, mirrors,
liquid silicone at -20°C, turf, plants, 320 x 1,270 x
543 cm (10 ft 6 in. x 41 ft 7 in. x 17 ft 10 in.).
Photograph: Attilio Maranzano. Courtesy: Jay
Joplin/White Cube, London. © the artist.

p. 150 Tadashi Kawamata
Born 1953 in Japan.
Les chaises de traverse, 1998
Installation view: the Hôtel Saint-Livier, Metz &
Synagogue of Delme. Commissioned by Fonds
régional d'art contemporain de Lorraine and
Synagogue de Delme. Photograph: Leo van
der Kleij.
Courtesy: Frac Lorraine.

p. 151 Rosemarie McGoldrick
Lives and works in London.
What Katy Did, 1999
Steel, wire, cable, speakers, recorded sound. View
of installation for the exhibition 'Day for Night', six
projects in Portakabin buildings: the Museum of
Installation, London. Photograph: Edward
Woodman. Courtesy: the artist and the Museum of
Installation, London.

p. 152 (above, above left + left) Loriot/Mélia
François Loriot and Chantal Mélia born 1947
in France.
Le Leurre et L'agent du Leurre, 1994–2000
Ready Made in China, 2000
Le Diable Probablement, 1993–2000
Installation views: the Museum of Installation,
2000. Photograph: David Grandorge.
Courtesy: the artists and the Museum of
Installation, London.

p. 153 Bob & Roberta Smith
Paint it Orange, 1997
Mixed media, videos and painted signs. Installation
view: 'Don't Hate Sculpt' exhibition: Chisenhale
Gallery, London. Courtesy: the artist and
Chisenhale Gallery, London.

p. 154 (below) Sarah Lucas
Born 1962 in UK (London).
Chuffing Away to Oblivion, 1999 (detail)
Newspapers, shellac, wood, door, picture rail,
light and linoleum, 110 x 281 cm (3 ft 7 in. x 9 ft
2 in.). Courtesy: Barbara Gladstone, New York.

p. 154 + 155 João Penalva
Born 1949 in Portugal (Lisbon); lives and works
in London.
From R., 2001
Video projection, furniture, painted cloths,
photographs, books and lights, dimensions
variable. Installation view: the Venice Biennale
2001. Photograph: Stephen White. Courtesy:
the artist.

p. 156 (above) Miguel-Angel Rios
Born 1943.
*Si me buscas...no me encuentras (If you look for me,
you will not find me.)*, 2001.
Courtesy: the artist.

p. 156 (below) Jeremy Wood
Born 1967 in UK; lives and works in London.
*The Map of Hope and Other Improbable
Locations*, 2002
Installation with video animation for exterior
projection, 35 mm mini DV film essay for monitor,
furniture arrangement & additional objects. Site:
empty rooms at the THU, Berlin, Germany.
Photograph: Gisela Dilchert. Courtesy: empty
rooms e.V., Berlin, Theater am Halleschen Ufer,
Berlin and the artist.

p. 157 (above) Joe Banks
Soundproofs, 1998
Installation view: the Museum of Installation,
London. Photograph: Edward Woodman. Courtesy:
the artist and the Museum of Installation, London.

p. 157 (below) Markus Wirthmann
Born 1963 in Germany; lives and works in Berlin.
*The Twentieth Century. Chapter V: The Total
Eclipse*, 2000
Theatre headlight, mirror ball, video camera and
monitor on mobile tripod system, mural
wallpaper, measurements variable. Installation
view: the Goethe-Institute Dakar, Senegal.
Courtesy: the artist.

p. 158 (left) Diana Thater
Born 1962 in USA San Francisco; lives and works
in Los Angeles.
Broken Circle, 1997
Interior view: the Buddenturm. Floor 2 (view B). 6
LCD video projectors, 1 video monitor, 7 laserdisc
players, 1 laserplay-2 synch, dimensions variable.
Courtesy: the artist and David Zwirner, New York.

p. 158 (right) A. K. Dolven
Born 1953 in Norway (Oslo); lives and works in
Lofoten and London.
Stairs, 2002
Video installation, digital video on DVD. Courtesy:
carlier/gebauer.

p. 158 (below) Eija-Liisa Ahtila
Born 1959 in Finland (Hämeenlinna); lives and
works in Helsinki.
Tuuli/The Wind, 2002
14 min. 20 seconds, 3-screen DVD. Installation
with sound, PAL 16:9, Dolby Digital 5.1. Edition:
5 + 1 ap, dimensions variable. View at Klemens
Gasser & Tanja Grunert Inc., New York.
Photograph: Mark Luttrell. © Crystal Eye Ltd.,
Helsinki. Courtesy: Klemens Gasser & Tanja
Grunert Inc., New York.

p. 159 Eija-Liisa Ahtila
Anne, Aki and God, 1998
Video installation, view at Klemens Gasser & Tanja
Grunert Inc., New York. © Crystal Eye Ltd.,
Helsinki. Courtesy: Klemens Gasser & Tanja
Grunert Inc., New York.

p. 160 Michael Petry
Born 1960 in USA (El Paso, Texas); lives and works
in London.
Contagion, 2000
Gardner Arts Centre, Brighton Festival 2000. 144
red crystal hearts, steel wire, rubber discs, red
theatre lights. Photograph: David Grandorge.

p. 161 (below) Catrin Otto
Born 1964 in Germany; lives and works in Berlin.
Full House, 1998
Various materials and cibachrome in aluminium.
Photograph: Jürgen Baumann. Courtesy: the artist
and empty rooms e.V., Berlin.

p. 161 (above) Gabriel Kuri
Born and based in Mexico City.
Momento de importancia, 2001
Conference table, chairs, green felt, microphones,
desk lamps, cold steam machine, blue walls,
ornamental plants, spotlights, water drinking unit,
dimensions variable. Courtesy:
Kurimanzutto, Mexico City.

p. 162 (left) Teresita Fernández
Born 1968 in USA (Miami); lives and works in
New York.
Bamboo Cinema, 2001
Acrylic, steel, 244 x 843 cm d. (8 ft x 27 ft 7 in. d).
Project commissioned by Public Art Fund.
Installation in Madison Square Park, April–Sept.
2002. Courtesy: the artist and Lehmann Maupin
Gallery, New York.

p. 162 (right) Daniel Guzmán
Born 1964; lives and works in Mexico City.
Untitled, 2000
Drawings, table, tablecloth, plant, dimensions
variable. International Studio Program, New York.
Courtesy: Kurimanzutto, Mexico City.

p. 162 (below) Bodys Isek Kingelez
Born 1948 in Kimbembele Ihuga; lives and works
in Kinnshasa, Congo.
Ville Fantome, 1996
Balsa, paper, cardboard, plastic, ink, misc.
120 x 170 x 240 cm (4 ft x 5 ft 6 in. x 8 ft).
Photograph: I. Kalkkinen & D. Dennehy. Courtesy:
the C.A.A.C, The Pigozzi Collection, Geneva.

p. 163 Karsten Bott
Born 1960 in Germany (Frankfurt am Main).
Von Jedem Eins (One of Each), 2001
Frankfurt. Courtesy: the artist

p. 164 (above) + 165 Bill Viola
Born 1951 in USA (New York); lives and works
in Long Beach.
Going Forth By Day, 2002
The Deluge, panel 3
The Voyage, panel 4
The First Light, panel 5
Video/sound installation, production stills.
Exhibiting site: Deutsche Guggenheim Berlin.
Photograph: Kira Perov. Courtesy: the artist;
Deutsche Bank and Solomon R. Guggenheim
Museum of Art.

p. 164 (below) Do-Ho Suh
Born 1962 in Korea (Seoul).
*Seoul Home/L.A. Home/New York Home/Baltimore
Home/London Home*, 1999
Silk and metal armaters, 378 x 609 x 609 cm
(12 ft 5 in. x 20 ft x 20 ft). Courtesy: MOCA,
Los Angeles.

the body of the audience

p. 169 Carlos Amorales
Born 1970 in Mexico; lives in Mexico City.
Funny 13, 2001
Wall paint, tape, sound system, devil suit.
Photograph: Philippe Boel. Courtesy: Galerie
Micheline Szwajcer, Antwerp.

p. 170 Christoph Draeger
Born 1965 in Switzerland (Zurich); lives and works
in New York.
Apocalypso Place, 2000
Dimensions variable. View at the Kunsthaus
Zürich, Biennale Torino, Italy
Photograph: Jules Spinatsche. Courtesy: the artist
and Galerie Anne de Villepoix, Paris.

p. 171 Aernout Mik
Born 1962 in The Netherlands.
Piñata, 1999
Video installation, digital video on DVD
edition of 2 + 1 a.p. Installation view: ARCO,
Madrid, 2000. Courtesy: carlier/gebauer.

p. 172 (above) Douglas Gordon
Born 1966 in UK (Glasgow); lives and works in Glasgow and New York.
Feature Film, 1999
35 mm film, still. View at the Atlantis Building, Brick Lane, London. Courtesy: Artangel, London.

p. 172 (below) Terry Smith
Lives and works in London.
Marking Time, 1999
Commissioned by Nuova Icona, Venice. 2 screen video. Installation view: the Cà Rezzonico Museum, Venice, Italy. Courtesy: the artist and Nuova Icona, Venice.

p. 173 (above) Eric Steensma
Born 1959 in The Netherlands (Alkmaar); lives and works in Amsterdam.
Roadshow, 2002
Projection/installation. *c.* 3 x 4 x 2 m (9 ft 10 in. x 13 ft 2 in. x 6 ft 6 in.). Courtesy: the artist.

p. 173 (below) Abigail Lane
Lives and works in London.
The Inspirator, 2001
Single-screen projector, fountain, mirror ball, dimensions variable. Photograph: Edward Woodman. Courtesy: the artist and Victoria Miro Gallery, London.

p. 174 (above) Eric Duyckaerts
Born 1953 in Belgium (Liège); lives and works in Paris.
How to Draw a Square, 1999
Paper board, pencil, DVD, video projector, 180 x 134 x 100 cm (6 ft x 4 ft 4 in. x 3 ft 3 in.). Courtesy: Galerie Emmanuel Perrotin, Paris.

p. 174 (below) Nicolas de Oliveira and Nicola Oxley
Live and work in London.
Burg Weogaran Dyreby, 1996–98.
Wood, polycarbonate mirrors. Courtesy: Peterborough Museum & Art Gallery and the artists.

p. 175 (above) Besnik and Flutura Haxhillari
Besnik Haxhillari born 1966 in Albania (Pogradec). Flutura Haxhillari born 1970 in Albania (Shkodra); both live and work in Canada.
Die Gulliver Träumen (Gulliver's Dreams), 1999
2 rocking capsules made from clear plexiglas, material bindings, photographs. Installation view: Kunstmuseum Basel, Switzerland. Courtesy: the artists and Galerie Knapp, Lausanne.

p. 175 (below) Santiago Sierra
Born 1966 in Spain.
Trabajadores que no pueden ser pagados remunerados para permanecer en el interior de cajas de cartón, 2000
Installation view: the Kunst Werke, Berlin, 2000. Courtesy: carlier/gebauer.

p. 176 Christine Hill
Born 1968 in USA
Volksboutique Organizational Ventures, 2002
Installation view Galerie für zeitgenössische Kunst, Leipzig. Photograph: Uwe Walter. Courtesy:

Galerie EIGEN+ART Berlin/Leipzig.

p. 177 Michael Landy
Break Down, 2001
C&A store Marble Arch, London. Photograph: Dillon Bryden. Courtesy: Karsten Schubert and Thomas Dane, London.

p. 178 + 179 Stan Douglas
Born 1960 in Canada (Vancouver); lives and works in Vancouver.
Journey into Fear: Pilot's Quarters 1 and 2, 2001
2 C-Prints (diptych), left and right side of diptych 71 x 89 cm (2 ft 4 in. x 2 ft 11 in.); 122 x 137 cm (4 ft x 4 ft 6 in.). Photograph: the artist, edition of 7. DOUST0220. Courtesy: the artist and David Zwirner, New York.

p. 180 (above) Olaf Nicolai
Born 1962; lives and works in Leipzig and Berlin.
Portrait of the Artist as a Weeping Narcissus, 2000
Polyester, 90 x 156 x 268 cm (2 ft 11 in. x 5 ft 1 in. x 8 ft 10 in.). Photograph: Uwe Walter, Berlin. Courtesy: Galerie EIGEN+ART Berlin/Leipzig.

p. 180 (below) John Bock
Born 1965 in Germany (Gribbohm); lives and works in Berlin.
Lombardi Bängli, 1999
Mixed media. Installation view: the Kunsthalle Basel, Switzerland. Photograph: Knut Klaßen. Courtesy: the artist, Klosterfelde Berlin and Anton Kern, New York.

p. 181 Christian Jankowski
Rosa, 2001
Production still. Courtesy: Klosterfelde, Berlin.

p. 182 (above) Sylvie Fleury
Born 1960 in Switzerland
Bedroom Ensemble II, 1998
Synthetic fur on wood, dimensions adaptable. Installation view Migros Museum für Gegenwartskunst, Zürich, 1998/1999. Photograph: A. Burger, Zurich. Courtesy: Galerie Hauser & Wirth & Presenhuber, Zürich.

p. 182 (below) Patrick Tuttofuoco
Born 1974; lives and works in Milan.
Walkaround, 2002
Installation in 10 parts; wood, aluminuim, plexiglas, paint and Neon Light. Site: Studio Guenzani, 2002. Photograph: Roberto Marossi, Milan. Courtesy: Gallery Guenzani, Milan (Private collection).

p. 183 Anne Laura Aláez
Born 1964 in Spain (Bilbao); lives and works in Madrid and New York.
Prostibulo, (Brothel) 1999
Mixed media. Courtesy: Galería Juana de Aizpuru, Sevilla/Madrid.

p. 184 + 185 (above) Hans Weigand
Born 1954 in Austria (Hall, Tirol); lives and works in Vienna.
Cotton, 2001
Artificial leather, steel, technical equipment, ink-jet print, *c.* 6 x 6 x 25 m (19 ft 7 in. x 19 ft 7 in. x 82

ft). Installation at the Museum Ludwig Köln, Cologne. Photograph: Alistair Overbruck. Courtesy: Gabriele Senn Galerie, Vienna.

p. 185 (below) Roman Signer
Born 1938 in Switzerland.
Kabine, 1999
Wood, acrylic paint, tin, detonator. Installation view: the Kunstmuseum St Gallen, Switzerland. Photograph: Stefan Rohner. Courtesy: Galerie Hauser & Wirth, Zürich.

p. 186 (above) Patrick Tuttofuoco
Velodream, 2001
Installation in 10 parts (vehicles), dimensions variable. S.M.A.K., Gent.
Courtesy: studio Guenzani, Milan.

p. 186 (below) Chinese Cartoon
Huang Yihan born 1958 in China (Lufeng Guangdong).
Xiang Ding Dang born 1973 in China Liang Jianbin, Su Ruoshan.
We are the Kids Who Never Grow Up, 2001
Installation by Huang Yihan, statues of children and flyings saucers. Courtesy: the artist.

p. 187 (above) Charles Long and Stereolab
Charles Long born 1958 in USA (Long Branch New Jersey). Stereolab founded 1991.
The Amorphous Body Study Center, 1995
Installation view Tanya Bonakdar Gallery, New York. Courtesy: Tanya Bonakdar Gallery, New York.

p. 187 (below) Charles Long
Holidays Situations, 1999
Installation view Saks Fifth Avenue, Beverly Hills, California. Courtesy: Shoshana Wayne Gallery, Santa Monica.

p. 188 Mariko Mori
Born 1967 in Japan.
Body Capsule, 1995
Beginning of the End, Shibuya, Tokyo, 1995
Courtesy: Galerie Emmanuel Perrotin, Paris.

p. 189 Thomas Eller
Born 1964 in Germany; lives and works in New York.
THE human re-entering nature, 2000
Silkscreen on aluminium, plants, 400 x 125 x 160 cm (13 ft x 4 ft x 5 ft 3 in.). Installation view: Echigo-Tsunami Triennial 2000, Japan. Photograph: S. Anza. Courtesy: the artist.

p. 190 (above) Vanessa Beecroft
Born 1969 in Italy.
VB46.026.ali, 2001
Vibricolor print 127 x 243 cm (4 ft 2 in. x 8 ft). Courtesy: Gagosian Gallery, New York.

p. 190 (below) Momoyo Torimitsu
Born 1967 in Japan (Tokyo); lives and works in New York.
Miyata Jira, 1997
Performance in New York. Courtesy: the artist and Jack Tilton Gallery, New York.

p. 191 (below) Gary Hill
Born 1951 in USA.
Viewer, 1996
Five-channel video installation (5 projectors,
1 five-channel synchronizer, 5 laserdisc players
and 5 laserdiscs edition of 2 and 1 artist's proof).
Courtesy: Gary Hill Studio and Donald Young
Gallery, Chicago.

p. 192 Tacita Dean
Born 1965; lives and works in London.
Fernsehturm, 2001
16 mm colour anamorphic film, optical sound,
44 min. Courtesy: the artist, Frith Street Gallery,
London and Marian Goodman Gallery, New York.

list of contributors

Research Co-ordination: Sotirios Bahtsetzis
Picture Research: Sarah Loriot
Administrative Assistant: Clare Fitzpatrick
IT Support: Kenichi Nakayama
Liaison: Rie Watanabe
Consultants: Sotirios Bahtsetzis, Jeremy Wood

With thanks to all contributing artists and
galleries, and to Robert Preece and Russel
Keziere for their support and advice.

index